time
for
joy

time for joy

DAILY AFFIRMATIONS

written by ruth fishel

illustrations by bonny van de kamp

Health Communications, Inc.
Deerfield Beach, Florida

www.bcibooks.com

Library of Congress Cataloging-in-Publication Data is available through the Library of Congress.

©1988 Ruth Fishel
ISBN 13: 978-0-932194-82-4
ISBN 10: 0-932194-82-6

Published by: Health Communications, Inc.
3201 S.W. 15th Street
Deerfield Beach, FL 33442

Cover design by Larissa Hise Henoch
Interior design and formatting by Dawn Von Strolley

This book is dedicated to Sandy Bierig, my partner,
who has helped me on my spiritual path
to JOY, a day at a time, and has spent a major part
of her life guiding so many other women
on their journey to recovery.

WITH GRATITUDE

I am deeply grateful to all the authors I have ever read who have been an inspiration to me and have held me up through the many curves and crevices and ups and downs that my life has taken.

I am grateful for all the people who have believed in me in the many years that I did not believe in myself.

I am deeply grateful again to Sandy Bierig for all the many, many hours of patience and help in editing this book to get it ready for submission; to my editor Marie Stilkind for her encouragement and inspiration and even her blue pencil working to prepare *TIME FOR JOY* for publication; and to Bonny Lowell for her wonderful and inspiring illustrations and for her friendship and encouragement, especially on days when I thought that I just could not write another page.

I especially want to thank and acknowledge the following people for the inspiring pages that they contributed: Sandy Bierig, Judy Costello, Diane Crosby, Roberta Hamilton, Maureen Lydon, Gary Seidler, Sandy Siraco, Marie Stilkind, Joyce Suttill, Barbara Thomas, Peter Vegso and Eileen White.

INTRODUCTION

One day, about two years after writing *The Journey Within: A Spiritual Path to Recovery*, I was taking a shower when I realized that I was only physically in the shower. My body was there but my mind was far away. It was solving . . . planning . . . and, something that I really knew I did not want to do anymore; it was still struggling.

And I remember yelling, "Where is the JOY?" "IT'S TIME FOR JOY!"

I came to the truth again that recovery is progress not perfection, and that I will never feel 100% great 100% of the time. Life changes and the more that I grow and change, the better I can handle the ups and downs that come my way. The more that I meditate and pray to come from a place of truth and love, and the more that I become willing to turn my life and my will over to a Power greater than myself, the more I am able to feel JOY in my life.

I was reinforced with the fact that recovery is on a daily basis. No matter how much we know, no matter how far we have grown, no matter who we are and what we do, recovery takes place in a 24-hour period and each day begins anew.

I need daily inspiration to feel close to my

1

Higher Power, to feel love, to feel peace. I must pray and meditate on a daily basis to continue to grow in my recovery. And I definitely cannot pass on any messages of love unless I feel love for myself.

Inspirational words have always been an important part of my life. I have been an avid reader since my childhood. I have always been moved by words. I have always felt the power of words, and from a very early age, I have been drawn to writing words that inspire the best in others.

Words can inspire, motivate and change us if we let them. I have experienced being lifted from a depression by inspiring, loving, moving words. Words can lift us to action. Words can move us to anger and rage or to love and tears. Most important, words can heal.

It is TIME FOR JOY for all of us! It is time to celebrate our recoveries and share them with the rest of the world! For all of us who are willing to grow and change, who have reached out and taken God's Gift of life and love, it is TIME FOR JOY!

Wherever you are at this moment, however far you have traveled to reach this point in time, may you know JOY. May this book be an inspiration for you when and as you need it. Read it by the page a day at a time or at random as you are so moved. Know that you are worthy of JOY, that you deserve to have JOY in your life. May you take this time to find your TIME FOR JOY and may you know peace and love.

I love you all!
Ruth

*T*oday I am on
my spiritual
path to recovery.

JANUARY 1

Wherever you are today is perfect. You have been on a journey arriving right here, right now in this moment in time and space. You are here to make a new beginning on your spiritual journey and to experience and accept JOY in your life. You are in a perfect place for spiritual growth and change. Everything you have done in your entire life has brought you to this very moment and it is perfect.

Accept yourself just as you are. All of yourself. Completely. Know that you are perfect and let yourself feel the joy of that knowledge.

Today I am on my spiritual path to recovery.

"The longest journey is the journey inward, for he who has chosen his destiny has started upon his quest for the source of his being."

Dag Hammarsjkold

We have often looked to other people, places and things for our answers and for our happiness. We thought others could free us from pain, fear or guilt. This has never brought any permanent happiness and in the long run we have not changed.

It is time to begin to trust that small voice within, coming from the person we really are. It is time to look within and begin to uncover all that has been blocking us from our truth, from our Higher Power. It is time to discover ourselves.

I am beginning to trust myself.
I am beginning to discover that I am okay.

"Some days I realize that many things can fragment my life. Then I can forget the focus and find I am agitated and nervous. Now I know that these feelings are a signal to sit and rest. During the quiet I can go inside and calm and restrengthen myself."

Eileen White

Today my body guides me to refocus and God heals me deep within as I again become strong and free.

7

"For there is . . . time . . . for every purpose."

Ecclesiastes

So many of us rushed year after year, constantly searching outside of ourselves, turning this way or that way, twisting ourselves inside out.

It is time to slow down
until you can stop.
Feel the peace of the moment.

This is your TIME FOR JOY!
Know that it is here and now.

"Courage is fear that has said its prayers."

So many times we have listened to the voices that go on in our heads and have been afraid to move forward. These voices might originally have come from our parents, teachers, friends or other people who have spoken to us out of their own fears and insecurities. We have, unknowingly, recorded them in our memories as our own.

Other times it has been our own fear and self-doubt that has blocked us from growth and change. It is time to trust a power greater than yourself today to guide you on your journey. It is time to let go and let God.

Today I am willing to let go and
let God work in my life. I am getting
my self-will out of the way.

Even when I have doubt, I know that a power greater than myself is guiding me on my path today.

JANUARY 7

How many times have you thought of changing something, getting a better job, a new house or going on for a higher education, and then found that nothing ever came of it?

Today it is time to let powerful, positive affirmations take over and encourage us to make positive changes in our lives.

I am worthy of positive changes today.

JANUARY 8

I do not need to know anything about this day beyond this moment. This moment is perfect . . . just as it is and I can handle anything in this moment. My Higher Power gives me all the strength I need today to handle whatever comes up in this moment.

Sometimes a small stirring, an uncomfortable feeling comes into our stomachs and we don't always know what the cause is and we want it to go away. We don't want to hear what it is telling us.

Other times a truth yells at us so loudly that we can't avoid hearing it and we know that it is time for change and that scares us, too. We want the feeling that the new knowledge creates to go away also. Even though we know that change will be better in the long run, the idea of change itself is what is most frightening.

For too long many of us tried to make those feelings go away with alcohol, food, drugs, sex and other dependencies. Even daring to listen to and begin to trust our inner voice is a new and rare experience for most of us in recovery.

I dare to listen to my inner voice
with a new trust today.

"You will learn to listen solidly to the voice within you and to follow only the path of joy."

Ramtha

It IS time for JOY!

As you learn the process of quieting the voices and old tapes that are running around in your mind, you will begin to be in touch with new truths from within, new feelings, new urges.

And as you begin to trust the ones that guide you toward growth and change, toward good and love, you will learn to discard those that come from fear and anger.

As you allow yourself to listen to and follow this new voice, JOY will fill your life and you will never go back to the old blocking ways.

Today I am trusting the urge to move ahead . . . to grow. . . to risk new directions.

*I am listening to the voice of truth
and love today.*

Whatever you see today, know that it is there. Do not try to make it better or worse than what it is. Whatever you see . . . whatever you feel is real. It is your reality. And as you learn to accept it without judgment and without resistance, tension will be released, struggle will disappear . . .

. . . AND YOU WILL KNOW JOY.

Today I am willing to let go of all my fear
so that I can find out what is real in my life.
I will take whatever comes without judgment.
I am ready to release all my resistance and
struggle so that I can find the good and
truth inside me.

"There are days when I doubt . . . myself . . . others . . . God . . . Trust will replace doubt if I am patient and easy on myself."

Maureen Lydon

I celebrate myself today and know that my feelings are okay. I am me, unique and alive.

"*When we discover the still, quiet place that lies within each of us, we can see it as a base to untangle ourselves from the doubt, indecision, ill health, guilt and other forms of old programming that result in confused and defused actions.*"

Hallie Iglehart

Miracles begin to happen when we sit still and begin to look within. Let those miracles be there for you today.

As you dare to see that you have been ruled by old programming, know that new programming, positive healthy programming, is taking its place. Know that you are in the process of clearing up and moving forward.

I am clearing out old confusion and doubt so that I can see the miracles today.

I celebrate myself today. I am alive. I am growing. I am willing to do all I am able to do to be the best of who I am.

We wandered so far, thinking happiness was somewhere else. Some of us went through so many people, always looking for the right one or ones who would have our answers. We put so much into our bodies, thinking that it would make us feel good. And we tried so many experiences, trying to hold on to the excitement and fun it might once have brought us.

Now we learn to slow down. And we learn a new truth.

Stop for a moment and think "JOY". And let that thought pour over you. Stop for a moment and think "LOVE" and let those feelings pour over you. Wherever you are, whatever you are doing, at any time in any day, just stop for a moment. You will find GOD and JOY and LOVE. Whatever you choose to think, to feel, to have, to be . . .

. . . is yours
whenever you choose it.

Today I take the time to be with me
and find peace and love and truth.
It is mine if I just stop. It is mine if I just
think the thoughts I want to feel.

"Now there is silence. Seek no further."

A Course in Miracles

As we meditate today our minds will begin to be still. Thoughts will come in and they will disappear. They will come in and the times that they disappear will be greater. The stretches of peaceful times will be longer. The peace you will feel will be deeper.

You are beginning to be in charge of your life. In this peace there is everything.

Today I am not afraid of the silence. I find peace in this silence and I am able to listen to God's will for me.

"*Most people fail because they do not wake and see when they stand at the fork in the road and have to decide.*"

Erich Fromm

trust   peace   faith

My Higher Power guides me today. I can move forward with the faith and trust that I am being lovingly led along the way, a step at a time, a day at a time.

JANUARY 19

We no longer have to block the truth because of our fears, doubts and insecurities. When coming to a new place of self-knowledge, we no longer need to anesthetize ourselves with our addictions.

We can stay awake and choose to make healthy decisions for ourselves today.

My Higher Power guides me in making all healthy and positive decisions today.

JANUARY 20

"We will want the good that is in all of us, even in the worst of us to flower and to grow. Most certainly we shall need bracing air and abundance of food. But first of all we shall want sunlight; nothing much can grow in the dark. Meditation is our step out into the sun.

Twelve Steps and Twelve Traditions,
Alcoholics Anonymous

As we quiet our minds to listen to our Higher Power, light begins to pour over all the dark places within and we are able to see the truth that has laid buried for years. We never had a chance to blossom in that darkness.

Today as we gently begin to discover who we are and accept ourselves just as we are, we will feel lighter and warmer and more relaxed.

I choose to live in the light of my truth today.

"We turn to teachings and practices of the great spiritual traditions when the time is right. The urge towards liberation is natural, and it often seems inevitable. We simply want to help ourselves live more fully, and we want to help others do the same."

Chop Wood, Carry Water

As I continue to grow on my spiritual path to recovery, I bask in the miracles of transformation and healing that are taking place in my life today.

JANUARY 22

*I deserve wonderful things to
happen in my life today.*

JANUARY 23

We were lost and could not feel anything but pain. Life no longer had a meaning. As far as many of us were concerned hope and faith had left a long time ago.

God has only been a prayer away. And as we were finally beaten to our knees, surrendering to God's will, not ours, the miracle of finding a power greater than ourselves in recovery began to give life a new meaning. Hope and faith returned.

I let God guide me in my recovery today,
knowing all decisions that come from good
and love will bring me joy.

"The truth waits for eyes unclouded by longing."

Tao to Ching

Accept all that you see. Accept yourself totally as you are.

This is the beginning of wisdom.

Today I will accept all of me just as I am.
I will put aside all judgments and I will
rejoice in the miracle of my uniqueness.

"Stop being limited by who we think we are."

Ram Dass and Paul Gorman

As we quiet our minds and begin to look within, we are going to hear voices, old tapes, that have been stumbling blocks to our self-fulfillment.

We have taken on those voices as our own. It is time to release them. It is time to let them go. Know that every negative tape you hear comes from the past. It has no part in the reality of today.

Right now, in this now, you have a choice as to what you are going to think. You are in charge of your thoughts. You are in charge of your present. You are in charge of your future.

Your Higher *Power is guiding the way.*

As I go about my day I trust all my decisions to my positive inner guide. Nothing from the past will block me or hold me back. Today is mine to use for growth and recovery. I love myself today.

JANUARY 26

Nothing can stop me from growing today!

"Meditation is a form of acknowledging your connection with the spirit of universal love, and it allows a sense of peace and love to flood your being. The tranquility that follows stays with you, reducing stress and promoting a state of awareness throughout the day."

Ruth Ross

As we quiet our minds, we get in touch with the universal energy that is within us.

As we let ourselves relax and let stress leave our bodies, we open up to more and more tranquility and peace. The more we open and let go of our stress, the more room we make to be filled with peace and love, and we carry that with us throughout our day.

———

As I stop today and take the time to be still, I become in touch with my Higher Power. I feel myself filling with love and peace as I relax and let go of the stress in my day.

*As I take the time to let my stress go today
I will be filled with love and joy and peace.
I will be aware of these feelings throughout
my day and share them with others.*

"I don't think we can postpone meditation until we move or clean the garage."

Eknath Easwaran

The 20 minutes or so twice a day that we take to meditate adds hours of energy and freedom and peace to our day.

Today I will treat myself to quiet time. Today I will be gentle with myself as I let myself do nothing but be who I am. Today I will value what I THINK.

"Sought through prayer and meditation to improve our conscious contact with God, seeking only the knowledge of His will for us and the power to carry it through."

Step Eleven *Twelve Steps and Twelve Traditions*

For those of us familiar with the 12 steps of recovery, many of us have thought that this step was at the end of recovery and that we would not be ready for it for a long time. Meditation especially seemed too foreign, too different.

There is no right or wrong way to pray and meditate as long as it brings you closer to your true spirit. Sitting quietly, bringing your attention to your breathing is only one way. Thousands of books have been published on this subject and you will find the right approach for you.

———

Today I give myself permission to take the quiet time I need to meditate and to improve my conscious contact with God.

". . . a joy will open our hearts like a flower, enabling, us to enter the world of reality."

Thich Nhat Hanh

As we continue to discover and release the blocks that have been holding us back and controlling us, we will know something is very different. We may feel lighter physically. Skin problems may clear up. Physical illness may begin to disappear. A new kind of self-confidence may suddenly appear and surprise us as it takes the place of old fears.

I will take the time I need for me today
to be quiet and listen to my Higher Power
as I gently make new discoveries
and gain new wisdom.

"Recovery is a path . . . not a sudden landing."

Sandra Bierig

I know that one step at a time I am making progress today. I am grateful for all my growth even if it is not always very obvious.

FEBRUARY 2

Once we became willing to change, once we were ready to look within to find our truth, lights began to shine for us on our path to recovery. But one light at a time . . . one step at a time.

Slowly . . . very slowly . . . we begin to see what has been holding us back . . . what our stumbling blocks have been.

Slowly and painfully we learn to let go of the power that the past and the fear of the future has over us and we learn to deal with and live in the now.

Layer after layer is uncovered as we continue to grow, as we continue to recover, a day at a time.

As I gently pull back each layer that has been blocking me from being the best of who I am, I dare look a bit further and then a bit further yet. I know that I am not alone on this path and God is guiding me every inch of the way.

FEBRUARY 3

"We cannot leave the trap until we know that we are in it. We are in a needless imprisonment."

Marilyn Ferguson

Life has a way of going on and on and on, and unless we begin to take charge, we stay the victims of everything and everyone around us.

We stay stuck in the same ruts that keep us reactors instead of actors.

I am no longer a victim of my past.
I am free to move in new directions today.
I am at choice in my life.

FEBRUARY 4

*Today I dare look within to see what is keeping
me stuck. I know I cannot change unless I know
what there is to change. I feel energized
and empowered to move forward.*

FEBRUARY 5

"For we are actually pioneers trying to find a new path through the maze of tradition, convention and dogma. Our efforts are part of the struggle to mature the conception of relationships between men and women—in fact all relationships. In such a light, every advance in understanding has value. Every step, even a tentative one, counts."

Anne Morrow Lindbergh

We slowly begin to do things our way and not the way of our parents and others important in our past. We gradually dare to make our own mistakes and grow in the knowledge that this is the only way we are going to learn. No one has been on our own particular path, although others have sought the same goals. There are no road maps, no guarantees.

_____

Today I dare to walk a new path where comfort and security are not my goals. I dare to reach out to my fellow human beings and become part of a society whose aim is peace and love and joy and recovery.

"Genuine beginnings begin within us, even when they are brought to our attention by external opportunities."

William Bridges

Until we have been ready to accept that we had to give up unhealthy addictions and dependencies, recovery was not possible. As long as we had depended on people, places and things to make us feel better, life held no hope.

Gradually these people, places and things began to fail us. They no longer made us feel better. In fact, they no longer worked in our lives at all.

We were forced to the truth that we had to change. We were brought to our knees in pain. We had to look within or stay miserable.

I am slowly finding new strength within me
as I begin to trust my inner voice.
I dare listen and take new risks
as I follow my inner path.

"A flower falls even though we love it. A weed grows even though we don't love it."
Dogen

Life is what it is. People are who they are. All the wishing and trying and struggling cannot change this.

We tried to change everything with our addictions and compulsions and obsessions. We tried to make everything the way we wanted it so that we could feel good. We tried to make people do what we wanted them to do so we could be happy.

The closer we come to accept what is here . . . what is real . . . what is true, whether we like it or not, the closer we will be to finding JOY.

I feel my entire body unwinding and relaxing as I give up my resistance and struggle. Today I accept life as it comes and learn to flow with it with peace.

"Am I willing to unlearn my tensions?"

Amy Dean

Picture all the things happening in a normal day that would make you uptight enough to clench your fist, perhaps when people respond rudely or when it rains on your parade.

As soon as we are willing to change our negative thoughts, our entire body will relax and we will feel PEACE.

Today I am willing to let go of all my thoughts and opinions that are negative and destructive in my life.

"To thine own self be true; and it shall follow as the night the day, thou canst not then be false to any man."

William Shakespeare

We are learning to listen to our intuition, to our own still quiet voice inside. We are learning to hear our truth, and in this process to love ourselves. There will be times that our friends will let us know that they think we should act in a different way.

Listen to their advice and think about it.

Then trust your own inner voice. It does not always sing in unison with others. But it does sing your truth so that you can live in peace with yourself.

Today I have the courage to follow my own
inner voice that I hear in prayer and meditation.
Today I dare to be true to myself
and my own needs, whether
anyone agrees with me or not.

Today I will look inside for my answers. Today I will trust my instincts and my connection to my Higher Power.

Today I am aware that all my negative feelings have been taped in my memory from people and events from the past. They no longer serve a purpose in my today. I am willing to let them go. I am willing to be free today to live in today. I am willing to experience what today has to offer without being colored by yesterday's feeling.

Even in moments of doubting I know that
my Higher Power is guiding me
on my path today.

FEBRUARY 12

"The key to a passionate life is to trust and follow the energy within us. "

Shakti Gawain

As we begin to slow down . . . to quiet our minds . . . to discover our blocks and not resist them . . . energy that has been blocked by our fear, resistance and denial begins to be released.

Trust this new energy that is emerging. It is your spiritual truth, your inner voice, your intuition.

As I let go of all the negative tapes that block my truth, I trust and follow the energy that leads me to peace and joy.

"As meditation deepens, compulsions, cravings and fits of emotion begin to lose their power to dictate our behavior. We see clearly that choices are possible; we can say yes or we can say no. It is profoundly liberating."

Eknath Easwaran

As we become more familiar with meditation, the easier it is to trust what we think, feel and remember.

And the more our trust deepens and we let things happen just as they are, the more we begin to develop acceptance.

Trust and acceptance are the beginning of choice.

Today my faith and confidence grow as I learn to accept all that I discover without judgment. I feel energy and life flowing through me with this new freedom.

"Love is the miracle cure. Loving ourselves creates miracles in our lives."

Louise Hay

When we can actually feel love for ourselves, when we can reach through all the layers and layers to uncover that feeling, miracles will happen in our lives.

To reach that special place inside is truly a miracle.

When we know that we are worth loving ourselves, then we will know everything.

I am beginning to actually feel the energy of love that I have inside. My entire being is in the process of being transformed with love.

FEBRUARY 15

Today I will "act as if" I am worth loving. I will begin by telling myself that I am worthy of loving myself. I will acknowledge all the good and lovable things about me. I will "act as if" until I know that it is true.

Today I am letting go of all my tensions and stress. Today I am willing to live in the moment and experience the JOY of the NOW.

Today I am letting myself feel peaceful.

Today I know that every breath that I take connects with all the energies of the universe and when I bring my attention to that moment of my breath, I will feel peace.

Peace and relaxation flow through me
with every breath that I take.

All times are not pleasant, happy times. As we well know, roses do have thorns and there is darkness before the dawn. At those times it can be easy to let ourselves sink into doubt and despair, sometimes even wondering if there really is a Higher Power guiding us.

It takes practice and discipline to develop a faith when things do not go our way.

Even in moments of doubt I know that my Higher Power is guiding me on my path today.

FEBRUARY 18

"Today I am establishing rapport with myself."

Peter Vegso

Rarely is meditation free from thought. Long-time meditators have thoughts. Meditation is full of distractions and surprises, just as life is full of distractions and surprises.

As we learn to let our thoughts be as they are in meditation, we learn to let life be what it is when we are not meditating. The easier that we can accept our thoughts, the easier we learn to accept what comes up in life.

Being gentle with ourselves in meditation gives us practice with being gentle to ourselves all day.

―――――――――

Today I know that I am doing the best that I can and will be gentle with myself. I will watch what comes without struggle and will accept what is and adjust myself to it, rather than wanting it to be different than it is.

FEBRUARY 20

"You are going to find a star to light your path."

A Course in Miracles

I know that I am being led along a path of healing today. As I become more and more open to spirituality and recovery, my path becomes brighter and clearer every day.

"You will find your strength within you; in places deep inside that you have not yet dared to visit. Know that you have all that you need to do all that is good and right in your life today."

Ruth Fishel

It is exciting to know that I have all the strength I need today to do all that is good and right in my life.

So many of us only knew what we felt and thought to be true. Our perceptions of ourselves were so very unrealistic. We had covered the beautiful person that we really were inside of us by layers of guilt and shame, self-loathing and self-disgust, pessimism and depression. We came to a place where we were so defeated and worn that we almost gave up thinking we could ever be any better.

We thought we were weak and that we couldn't handle life. We thought we had to lean on others for strength.

As we grow in recovery, we are finding out that a truly beautiful person has been under all those layers and has been just waiting to be discovered. This person has strength that has not been tapped. And all we have to do is ask our Higher Power to guide us, to show us we have all that we need today.

God is guiding me on my path to self-sufficiency and independence today. As I become willing to let go of my feelings of inferiority and weakness, my Higher Power gives me all the strength I need for all that comes up for me today.

"We have met the enemy and they is us."

Pogo—Walt Kelly

Up until now we have thought our problems were everything else but us. Today we are learning that we are our own worst enemy.

This knowledge opens up the world for change and growth. Know this without fear. Know this without judgment. Know this with relief.

Finally . . . changes can occur.

Finally . . . we are on our spiritual journey to recovery.

Today I have the courage to own my own unhappiness, daring to look within to discover its source. Today I treat myself as a friend with gentleness and acceptance.

"'And what is as important as knowledge?' asked the mind. 'Caring and seeing with the heart,' answered the soul."

Flavia

I am growing in my ability to trust what feels good and right. Today I can look within and wait until I know with my heart.

Inside each of us is a very beautiful place. It is a special place where we really live. It is where we find our truth and God's Will for us.

We find that place when we quiet our minds in meditation. We find that place when we quiet our minds and look within, listening with our hearts, not with our minds.

By taking the time to begin our day in this manner, all the rest of our 24 hours will be influenced spiritually. We can continually tap into this peace and quiet that is only a breath away.

I will give myself the gift of time today
to be quiet and hear with my heart.
I will go to my special place inside
where I really live in love and in joy
and carry those feelings with me
throughout the day.

It feels so safe to know that there is always a special place within me where I can feel peace.

FEBRUARY 27

"We come to believe that life has always involved traffic jams and air pollution."

Rabbi Kushner

If we have lived with traffic jams all our lives, how do we know that quiet roads exist?

If we have lived with only polluted air, how do we know that there is pure, fresh healthy air anywhere on this planet?

By beginning to trust ourselves and the goodness of the universe, we begin to know that what feels wrong is wrong. What goes against our instinct for goodness and truth is not goodness and truth for us.

Once this begins to come clear, we will know we have choices and begin to look for them.

Today I will trust myself when something does not feel smooth and flowing. I will begin to look around for alternatives to anything that feels rough and irritating.

"We must never be blinded by the futile philosophy that we are just the hapless victims of our inheritance, of our life experience and of our surroundings—that these are the sole forces that make our decisions for us. This is not the road to freedom. We have to believe that we can really choose."

Bill Wilson

All that has happened before this very second is past. We have absolutely no control over it. All the thinking and praying in the world will not change it.

What is important is that we know right now that yesterday has no power over us any longer. Let yesterday serve as a light on all the lessons we no longer have to go through again.

I am at choice today. I accept the responsibility of my life with a new sense of maturity, confidence and even excitement.

MARCH 1

"When we really love and accept and approve of ourselves exactly as we are, then everything in life works. Its as if little miracles are everywhere."

Louise Hay

Today I will feel good about myself and accept myself just the way I am.
I am open and ready to discover all the miracles of this day.

MARCH 2

As the practice of meditation continues and deepens, we observe more and more the truth of who we are. Be sure that you do this without judgment. Simply be aware. Notice. Accept.

What you see is exactly who you are, and who you are is perfect for this time and this place.

Approve of yourself exactly as you see yourself. As you let go of energy tied up in judgment and criticism, new energy will be released for living. New energy will be released for positive change.

———————

Today I am letting go of all energy that is resisting the truth about me.
That energy is being replaced with positive and loving energy, and I am accepting that I am okay just the way I am. I am now open to see the miracle of love in my life.

"Do you want to be happy or do you want to be right?"

Gerald Jampolsky

So much energy is wasted when we try to win an argument, insist on proving our point, or try to convince the other person we are right. And when energy is depleted in this way, we certainly are not happy.

Take a few moments and remember what this arguing feels like in your body.

Now take a few moments and let your body remember and feel the release of letting go . . . of knowing you are right for you and it does not matter what anyone else thinks.

Today I will stop and ask, "How important is it?" When I find myself defending or trying to prove my point, I am in the process of learning to trust my own truth. When it feels right inside, I am seeing that it is all I need.

Where I am at this moment is perfect. My past is my friend today as I take the lessons that I can learn from it and say thank you. Everything that has brought me to this moment is a gift and I am a stronger and wiser person because of it.

my past

"Wanting is the urge for the next moment to contain what this moment does not. When there's wanting in the mind, the moment feels incomplete. Wanting is seeking elsewhere. Completeness is being right there."

Stephen Levine

I will never be in the now if I am waiting for the future. I will never be happy in the moment if I am wishing for something else. I will never be satisfied with a relationship or a friendship if I am waiting for the other person to change.

This is a new concept for many of us but once understood, it will bring great joy and peace to your TODAY.

Today I will accept what I have and what I am and what I see in this moment. I will be fully alive in this moment and feel the joy of knowing that it is all that there is right now.

MARCH 6

I am learning to trust my instincts and move away from unpleasant and stressful people, places and things. I no longer have to stay in situations that bring me unhappiness and pain. I am turning around today to see the joy.

"As you walk, you cut open and create that riverbed into which the stream of your descendants shall enter and flow. "

Nikos Kazantzakis

As we walk along our new path in recovery, learning, loving, discovering and beginning to trust our own inner truth, we feel joy in the knowledge that we are going in the right direction. We no longer need to listen to the voices in our heads that came from other generations, other's fear and ignorance, from another time and place.

I feel so good knowing that I am a power of example to future generations today as I walk on my new path of truth. I am making a difference not only in my own life but in the lives of those who follow me.

MARCH 8

I trust all that comes up for me today. I now know there is no value in hiding the truth from myself. I choose today to know everything about me and I am excited about this new adventure.

"Thoughts of your mind have made you what you are, and thoughts of your mind will make you what you become from this day forward."

Catherine Ponder

It is impossible to have two thoughts in your mind at the same time. As you bring your attention to your meditation, all other thoughts will fade away. Thoughts will come back, but they will fade away again. And they will come back and then leave.

This process will soon become a habit for you as you learn to bring attention to the moment. You will begin to notice the thoughts that come and go as you go about your everyday life. And you will begin to recognize your negative thoughts and how they affect you.

Today I know that I am in charge of the quality of my life. I am growing in the ability to become aware of the thoughts that have been controlling me.

"Each one of us who travels further than the obstacles will know a different kind of life from that time on."

J. Stone

*I am open and willing today to
take a step forward in a new direction.
I am no longer allowing myself to
stay stuck by old thoughts and feelings.
This new place is exciting and energizing.*

MARCH 11

Today I continue to let go of all thoughts that have been pulling me out of the present and bringing me to the past and future. I am becoming more and more open to let the power of good and love enter my life.

I can be centered and at peace inside when the world is going my way, as well as when things are happening that are not my choice. I am learning to focus on this newly found inner peace, especially at times of confusion and stress.

"*The need to grow, to change, to affect the world around us is part of God's plan for each of us. I will trust the urge. I will let it guide my steps.*"

Each Day a New Beginning

I have a purpose today. As I let go and let God, this purpose is becoming more and more clear. My heart is full of joy and love as I move more towards God's Will for me.

To accept ourselves as we are means to value our imperfections as much as our perfections."

Sandra Bierig

The inherent ability of human beings to grow means that they are not born perfect. Therefore to expect perfection of ourselves is to deny what makes us special, our humanness.

I will value myself today both for my perfections and especially for my imperfections.

"I have outgrown the need to suffer. "

Al-Anon Expression

*My Higher Power guides me in directions
that fills positive needs in my life today.
I have grown to see that my true needs
are love and peace and joy.*

*"It is exciting to know
that I am at choice today."*

It does not matter what is going on in my life on the outside. All that matters is how I choose to feel on the inside.

I have found tools today that can guide me on a positive path. All I have to do is use them.

Today I can choose whether to feel positive or negative.

---

*Choosing positive thoughts and making
positive choices fill me with new strength,
confidence and excitement. I can feel
positive energy flow through me
with every positive thought I choose.*

"You are a child of the universe, no less than the trees and the stars; you have a right to be here. And whether or not it is clear to you, no doubt the universe is unfolding as it should."

Desiderata
Max Ehrmann

Today I know I have a right to be alive and happy and full of joy. Today I trust that I am where I am supposed to be, and am moving in the right direction.

"Don't hide your light under a lampshade."

Today I will be part of the mainstream of life,
letting people see me as I am. I will share
what I have when it can be useful, looking
for opportunities to give to others
the best of who I am.

"Healing is accomplished the instant the sufferer no longer sees any value in pain."

A Course in Miracles

At some level pain has been a tool we have used to satisfy needs that we did not know how to meet in any other way. We might have learned at an early age that we would get love and comfort when we were sick. We then associated being sick with being loved.

These messages were recorded in our subconscious and continued to play while we were not aware of them. As this new awareness becomes real for us, we discover with JOY that there are healthy and positive ways to get our needs met.

Today I dare to openly express my needs and find healthy ways to get them met.
I like feeling good today. I like myself today.

MARCH 20

"The energy stays stuck as long as people are focusing on others as the problem or the solution."

Shakti Gawain

I am becoming more open to look within me today for my solutions. I trust that I will find the right answers if I go quietly within and follow my inner guide.

"If we are willing to examine the agitation of our minds and look just beyond it, we quite readily find entry into rooms that hold surprising possibilities, a great inner calm, sharper concentration, deeper intuitive understanding and an enhanced ability to hear one another's heart."

Ram Dass and Paul Gorman

God is guiding me in peace and in calm today. I know that anything that upsets this feeling is not permanent and will pass. I no longer allow upsets to keep me from seeing the good in others.

"Take the time to come home to yourself everyday."

Robin Casarjean

No matter how busy I am today, I will begin and end my day with quiet time. I look forward to that time when I stop all outward activity, rest and look within for my peace and truth.

"The admission that we don't know is the first step on our journey toward knowledge."

Chop Wood, Carry Water

When our pride finally allows us to admit that our way isn't working, when we can finally put aside our egos and look for help, truth begins.

Our struggle is over when we reach that wonderful, painful, joyful moment when we say, "I can't."

We become open to love and true relationships and spirituality.

We become open to peace.

Today I no longer struggle
to find my answers alone.
I welcome and am open to positive and
healthy support wherever I find it.

Forgiveness is no longer a choice in my life.
I have chosen the path to freedom.
I have chosen the path to truth.
I have chosen the path to JOY.

None of this is possible if I hold on to old resentments. None of this is possible if I hold on to my anger and self-pity. None of this is possible if I need to win and be right.

I forgive myself and all others today.

I am not in charge of today. Anything can happen today. It could be warm or cool, cloudy or sunny . . . it could even rain.

Life includes everything . . . the wind and the storms, as well as birth and death, and the sun and the rainbows.

There is no good or bad. There is life. As we begin to learn to accept each situation, pleasant or unpleasant, we will feel more and more alive in the NOW. Unpleasant situations will lose their power to make us miserable. We truly can be OKAY NO MATTER WHAT.

My Higher Power is with me in the sun
as well as the rain, in pain as well as joy. As long
as I know that I am protected and guided by the
power of faith and love, I will remain centered
and balanced through all of this day.

"Be still and know that I am God."

The Bible

Listening to God's voice within takes time and practice and patience. The only way we can hear it is to quiet our minds, to be still.

Sitting still, daring to be with ourselves in quietness is an extraordinary new experience for most of us.

The rewards are beyond your imagination.

God gives me all the willingness
I need today to sit quietly and listen.

I am good enough . . . just the way I am.

I am at choice today. I can watch my negative thoughts go by and replace them with positive thoughts of love and compassion.

MARCH 29

"The less you expect, the less you judge. The less you cling to this or that experience as significant, the further you will progress. For what you are seeking is a transformation of your being far beyond that which any specific experience can give you. It is important to expect nothing, to take every experience, including the negative ones, as merely steps on the path, and to proceed."

Ram Dass

When we can accept life on life's terms, when we stop looking for "the perfect family" or "the perfect mate," when we accept each individual as they are without judgment, then we will know peace.

God gives me all the strength and courage to accept whatever happens in my life today. It is so freeing to know that I am no longer a victim of people, places and things.

"Nothing has changed but my attitude. Every-thing has changed."

Anthony De Mello

*My Higher Power is guiding me
with my positive attitude today. Negatives are
no longer something I choose to live with.
I feel positive strength pour through me as
I release all negative thoughts.*

"I am not the victim of the world I see . . . What I see without, is a reflection of what I have first seen within my own mind. I always project onto the world my own thoughts, feelings and attitudes which preoccupy me. I can see the world differently by changing my mind about what I want to see."

Gerald Jampolsky
Love is Letting Go of Fear

*With softness and gentleness
I am turning around all negative thinking
so that my mind is positive.
It feels so good to be in charge of the world
that I am creating for myself.*

APRIL 1

*"Who you are is a necessary step
to being who you will be."*

Emmanuel

Have no regrets for who you are. Give lip service to the fact that you are perfect, even if you do not believe it. Every moment, every event, every experience that has formed and molded you had to take place for you to begin right here. . . right now . . . in this present moment.

You cannot go on to be who you want to become unless you have this starting point.

Accept yourself with joy and gratitude today and continue to develop to be the best of who you are.

---

*I accept myself today and am grateful
that I can grow from where I am. As I bring
more and more love to myself, I continue to
blossom and expand, growing
to be the best of who I can be.*

APRIL 2

There are days when I might have to sit back and wait. I might have to wait for the right time . . . the right energy . . . the right answer. There are days when I might even have to wait for the right person to take the other side of my burden so we can lift it together and get it through the door.

I cannot always have the energy that I want or the answers or the time or the right person in my life. These days are difficult.

These are the times to pause and rest. There are days when other people's energies are involved with my answers and they will fall into place in the right time and then I will know what to do.

Today I wait in peace and rest
in the knowledge that God
is working for me while I am resting.

I am open to positive changes in my life today.

"The moment before dawn is the darkest."

Author Unknown

There are days when it is difficult to stay positive. There are days when you feel like giving up. There are days that even a drink or a pill or a candy bar or any other destructive addiction might APPEAR to be your only answer.

STOP!

When life seems at its darkest . . . STOP. Call your sponsor. Ask for help. Pray. Meditate. Talk to SOMEONE HEALTHY AND POSITIVE.

HANG IN THERE!

Today I am hanging in no matter what.
Even when my conscious mind wants
to give up, I will reach for that healthy,
loving part deep within me and with
the help of prayer and meditation and the
good people in my life, I will find a rainbow.

"Stopping the mind does not bring wisdom, what brings wisdom is understanding the nature of the mind . . . mindfulness is the most powerful means of cutting through the hindrances. We can sit with any of them, and rather than blocking our meditation, they can become the object of the investigation."

Steven Levine

As we learn to bring awareness to what is going on in our minds, we begin to discover our truth. We begin to discover who we really are.

We no longer need to cover up our truth with alcohol or drugs or unhealthy dependencies and relationships. We know now that only by seeing who we are, where we have come from and where we are going, can we grow and be healthy.

Today I am open to all of who I am.
As I bring my attention to all of me, without judgment, I grow in wisdom and freedom.

APRIL 6

*Today I am breaking out
of old patterns, rewriting old tapes
and letting my life flow with love and joy.*

"If I lose my direction, I have to look for the North Star, and I go to the north. That does not mean that I expect to arrive at the North Star. I just want to go in that direction."

Thich Nhat Hanh

I am moving toward my goals today with just the right energy that I need. My progress will be perfect and I have the faith and trust that all the steps I take along the way will become clear when it is necessary.

We cannot expect to find peace and harmony in our lives if we are only looking for people who agree with us. The world consists of all types of individuals, each with their own perspective, each with their own individual opinions. If we find happiness only when someone agrees with us, our moments of peace and JOY will be very rare indeed.

We must learn to accept disagreement. We must learn to respect other points of view, other perspectives. We can find mutual harmony and peace if we can learn to agree to disagree. As we begin to learn this on a personal individual level, agreeing to disagree without a fight, without an argument, we can then begin to pass this lesson along to our friends and our neighbors, our family and our coworkers.

As we begin to accomplish this on a daily, individual basis, then we are contributing toward peace for all humanity.

Today I can find peace within myself without needing the approval and agreement of others. Today I can love and respect people who do not always share my view of the world.

APRIL 9

"And could you keep your heart in wonder at the daily miracles of your life, your pain would not seem less wondrous than your joy."

Kahlil Gibran

My heart is open to all that happens in my life today. There is such joy at being alive and feeling everything with a full and open heart.

*I am so grateful for the guidance
I have received in my recovery.*

*I am attracted to positive people
and I attract positive people to me.
Today I continue to seek and find people
who are positive, healthy and nurturing.*

"When you touch a fellow human being with love, you are doing God's work."

Emmanuel

The more I let go of my own suffering and self-pity, I can see those around me with the eyes of love and compassion. I am becoming more aware of other people's pain and unhappiness today and I will reach out to them in loving ways that heal me while I am helping to heal them.

APRIL 12

Today I know that everytime I inhale,
I am breathing in powerful healing energy.
And everytime I exhale, I am letting go.
I am letting go of all anxiety, all stress,
all negativity that is standing in the way of
my feeling good about myself.

APRIL 13

"No one succeeds without effort. Mind control is not your birthright. Those who succeed owe their success to their perseverance."

Ramana Maharshi

Wishful thinking does not put food on the table or advance our career. A lucky break at the lottery is one in a million and we cannot succeed if we are waiting for that to happen for us.

Sometimes it seems as if success takes place because of a lucky break or being in the right place at the right time. Usually the lucky break and the right time has been preceded by a history of hard work, positive thinking and being open and unblocked so that we can attract that which is positive and good for us.

Today I have faith and perseverance to stay on my path and do what is necessary whether or not it gives me immediate results and gratification. I am letting go of my impatience, procrastination, fear and doubt. I trust that God knows the right time for the right results.

"When we refuse air, light and food, the body suffers. And when we turn away from meditation and prayer, we likewise deprive our minds, our emotions and our intuitions of vitally needed support. As the body can fail its purpose for lack of nourishment, so can the soul."

Alcoholics Anonymous, World Service, Inc.

Today I am growing in my awareness that my mind, body and spirit need exercise and nourishment. Through prayer and meditation, exercise and inspirational reading, I am developing a personal program for physical, mental and spiritual growth.

"The resistance to the unpleasant situation is the root of suffering."

Ram Dass and Paul Gorman

It is only our judgmental mind that decides whether a situation is pleasant or unpleasant. We are not fortune-tellers. We are not God.

To accept what comes up as neither good nor bad, pleasant nor unpleasant but just what is, will release us from our resistance to life. We will then be open to experience life as an adventure and to learn to see beyond appearances.

I will put aside all judgments and
accept each and every situation
with openness and trust today.
Only then will I discover the joy
that lies beyond my fear.

*Today I picture myself flooded with the glow
of a powerful bright light that is guiding me
on my positive path of success and happiness.*

I have been given gifts which will make me feel fulfilled only when I have used them for others, as well as for myself. Keeping myself to myself is a waste of my ability to become truly whole.

I will open myself up to all the possibilities around me today, leaving my fear of change behind.

There comes a day when you might be tired and weary and wonder why you have no answers. There comes a time when all the work that you have done seems to be in vain. The road ahead looks so long and you have come so far, and there seems to be no end in sight.

On these days know that the road is not as it seems, that reality is just not clear today. The sun is always there, even if the clouds block you from seeing it.

Rest. Slow down. If at all possible, take the day off. And if you cannot do this, take some time to be very good to yourself today.

Be gentle. Rest and be renewed.

Have faith.

Today I need to do nothing more than pray and meditate. I trust that all the energies of the universe are working in my behalf. I can sleep comfortably in the knowledge that God is working when I am not.

"Learn to look at other human beings with the eyes of compassion."

Thich Nhat Hanh

If any negative feelings are triggered in me today, I will not act on my first impulse or desire. I will stop and get in touch with my breathing and my connections with the universe. I will take time to remember to see the other person's point of view.

There are days that do not always go the way we would like them to go. And we find out later that God's Will was not our own, even though we thought we were in complete alignment. When these days happen, as they will now and then, know that you are OKAY NO MATTER WHAT. Know today is not forever, that everything changes and flows . . . that this 24 hours is just what it is in this moment. And know that you can handle anything for a moment.

I can handle anything that comes
up today . . . even if it is only
for a moment at a time.

"If healing is about being whole, then every expression of being wants acknowledgment, including the things I don't like."

Dianne M. Connelly

It feels terrific letting go of perfection as my goal. As I let go of my judgments, all parts of me come together and I feel complete.

"If you cannot be compassionate to yourself, you will not be able to be compassionate to others."

Thich Nhat Hanh

Today I will be aware not to judge myself when I act less than perfect. I am beginning to love myself just as I am and that feels so nice.

*Today I can set my goals with the clear and
confident knowledge that I can only do one
thing at a time and take one step at a time
towards that goal. I do not need to wait until
I reach that goal to be happy and satisfied.
I am fulfilled with each step, knowing
that is all I can do in each moment.*

APRIL 24

"When you understand, you cannot help but love. You cannot get angry. To develop understanding, you have to practice looking at all living beings with the eyes of compassion. When you understand, you love. And when you love, you naturally act in a way that can relieve the suffering of people."

Thick Nhat Hanh

Today I am practicing looking at all beings with the eyes of compassion. Not only do I feel good when I come from a place of love and understanding, I also feel useful and connected.

APRIL 25

Positive energy attracts positive energy. Today my Higher Power continues to guide my growth so that I am more and more open. I am becoming free and unblocked and am attracting all that is good and right in my life.

APRIL 26

You have been working long and hard in your recovery. And you have come so far.

It is now time to try softer.

It is now time to be willing to let all the powers and energies of the universe work for you.

It is time for you to be open . . . to be willing . . . to allow those energies to carry you to your next step. It is time for JOY.

Today I am open to all the powers of the universe.
I am letting them work for me and carry me to my next step . . . JOY!

"Behold the turtle who makes progress only when she sticks her neck out."

For many years so many of us hid in our addictions or escaped into our fantasies. We withdrew when we did not like what we saw and shut down when life did not feel the way we wanted it to feel.

We no longer have to retreat, withdraw or escape. It is exciting to know that we are guided by a Power greater than ourselves. Today we have the courage to emerge from our shell to take risks and live. We are strengthened by each new risk, even if it does not always turn out exactly the way we had planned. We are learning that we get nowhere by retreating or standing still. God has a plan for us far greater than we can image for ourselves. We have to be present to experience it.

Today I have the courage to face life as it is
and make progress a part of my life.
I am willing to take chances and
grow and risk and feel what it
means to be fully alive in the moment.

*"You have to take it as it happens
but you should try to make it happen
the way you want to take it."*

Old German Proverb

Once something has occurred, the only way I can take responsibility for how I feel is to adjust my attitude toward it.

As my thinking becomes more and more positive, as I become more open to the positive energies of the universe, and as I continue to draw positive people to me by my own thoughts and actions, life will become more and more what I want it to be.

It is exciting to know that my thoughts and my actions in the present moment condition the next moment. I am responsible for my future. Today I am bringing awareness to my self-talk and replacing all negative thoughts with positive thoughts as soon as they appear on my mindscape.

With every breath that I take,
healing is taking place
whether I am aware of it or not.
I relax safely in the knowledge that
positive, healing energy is working
in my life today. I am being renewed
and refreshed and energized.

As I start this day with quiet meditation,
I feel myself becoming still and at peace.
At any time during the day I can bring my
mind back to this moment. I will bring my
attention and awareness back to the peace that
I have when I am with my breath and I know
that my breath is with me at all times,
whether I remember it or not.

As I begin to accept life on life's terms, I begin to know the joy of accepting all of me as I am. Then I become more and more willing to let go of all that is not positive and loving in life today. I am coming to know that I do deserve happiness and fulfillment and that love begins with myself.

When I look within, I find I have all that
I need. It feels wonderful to discover that
I already am the beautiful person
that I would like to be.

The thought of change often brings up great fear. And fear of change leads to resistance to change. Even though we know that things could be better by being different, it is very hard to let go of the known. We usually prefer what we know to what we don't know, even when what we know is not pleasant.

Therefore, it often takes great pain for us to change. A crisis can precipitate change.

As we grow in recovery and faith, we need not wait for another crisis to make a decision to change or grow. As we spend more time meditating and looking within and become in touch with our truth, we can make small changes on a daily basis that lead to bigger changes over a longer period of time.

Today I am open to making small changes in my life that lead me, a step at a time, on my spiritual path to recovery. I have faith in the guidance that I am receiving. I trust that I will know intuitively when the time is right for these changes.

"Life itself cannot give you joy unless you really will it. Life just gives you time and space. It's up to you to fill it."

Author Unknown

It is beautiful to know that I am the creator of the way I think and feel today, that I can choose my now. Today I choose to feel joy and I will do all that I have to do to make that possible!

MAY 4

"You are the only person who thinks in your mind. You are the power and authority of your world. . . . You get to have whatever you choose to think."

Louise Hay

Today I choose to think positive and loving thoughts.I know that if I do this I will feel loving and positive and create a positive and loving world for myself and those around me.

MAY 5

"If your eyes are blinded with your worries, you cannot see the beauty of the sunset."

Krishnamurti

Worry forms a box and keeps us stuck in it. When we stay with our fears and our concerns, they box us in, physically, emotionally and spiritually. They become blocks to all our senses. They keep us from feeling anything else. We cannot hear, see, smell, touch or speak of anything positive.

We are closed to joy and love. We are stuck.

Today I will let my Higher Power handle my worry so that I can be free. I choose to be alive in this moment and not blocked by the conversations that go on over and over in my head.
I will stop trying to figure everything out and will trust that I will get the right answers at the right time.

*"Consciousness is like a river, and your whole
self . . . including every cell of your body is con-
tinuously being fed by it . . . Just as your body
lives by the flow of blood that carries the substance of food to every cell, so is your whole self
being sustained through the substance of thought
emanating from the flow of consciousness."*

Ramtha

*Today I feel my entire body energized by my pow-
erful, positive thoughts. I feel alive and full of joy
as I feed myself with loving and positive energy.*

*"I don't always want to feel
what I feel . . . But I do.
I don't always want things to be
what they are . . . But they are."*

There are certainly times, no matter how hard I work on my recovery and growth, that I am going to feel what I don't want to feel.

As soon as I accept that this is part of life and allow it to be as it is, I can be just as open to the joy and happiness.

------

*Today I choose to accept life
on its terms . . . all of it.
I am open to all I see, hear, think
and feel in the moment, without resistance.
I am open to being fully alive and
enjoying the adventure.*

*I am letting go of all self-criticism today
and changing all my judging thoughts
to thoughts of love. I am becoming softer
and more gentle and accepting of myself
making more space to feel love and joy.*

"Pain alone was not the enemy; the real enemy is fear and resistance."

The Buddha

We sought to avoid pain at any length. We thought a few drinks or a few joints, pills, candy bars, new jobs, romances, sex, relationships, etc., etc., etc., would ease the pain and bring us joy. You name it. We were willing to try it. Anything to make the pain go away.

And we did not even know that it was peace we were looking for; we thought we just wanted relief from our pain. We resisted in every way we knew because we were so afraid of our pain.

To discover that PAIN DOES GO AWAY when we give up our resistance to it is indeed a miracle! To experience the freedom and JOY that comes when we dare look and accept the truth around us is worth every moment we have lived to this very moment.

Today I am letting a power greater than myself remove all my fear. I am now free to look within for my answers.

MAY 10

"Lord make me an instrument of Thy peace . . ."

St. Francis of Assisi

*Today I will look for opportunities to continue
to grow through seeing the beauty
around me and in me.*

*Today my trust in the overall and the long
run is deep within me and growing.
When events and people do not act as I would
like them to act, I reach deeper inside
for my faith and let it comfort me.*

"If you can, help others; if you cannot do that, at least do not harm them."

Randy Rind
Quoted in *Chop Wood, Carry Water*

There are times when we are very needy and we do not think we have anything to give to others. There are times when we have to take from others, and this is fine.

Sometimes we are so caught up with our own needs that we become insensitive to the needs of others. The old way was to be on automatic pilot and react and lash out, taking our moods and frustrations out on others.

As we grow in awareness, we learn to think before we act, knowing that we can be in charge of our actions and choose to come from good, even when we don't want to.

———

When I place myself in the hands and heart of my Higher Power today, I know that I will get my needs met. Only then do I trust that I will come from good and love, keeping the good of others in my mind and heart.

"If we have to determine which of two courses to take, we ask God for inspiration, an intuitive thought or decision. Then we relax and take it easy, and we are often surprised how often the right answers come after we have tried this for a while."

Bill Wilson
Alcoholics Anonymous

When I find myself with a choice today, I will not act out of haste. I have a new faith and trust today. I am learning that when I take the time to quiet myself, answers come that are right for me.

Meditation is where I listen for those answers. Letting go of my own fears and doubts and insecurities allows me to open my channels to hear and to know. All my answers come when I trust in my Higher Power, in goodness and love and truth.

Today I will wait in quiet and faith for a clear answer before making any decisions. Today I feel secure, trusting that my instincts are guiding me on every step on my path.

*I have all the power I need today to
say no to negative choices. The personal
choices I make today are positive and healthy.
I take responsibility for my life today.*

"Our own creative energy is waiting to move through us once we get out of our own way. Cleansing the mind of negative thought, quieting the chatterer and becoming one with the moment provides the environment for this energy to flow through us."

Ruth Ross

We are all born with a pure spirit, full of love and goodness and creative energy. Each negative experience, each reaction, each negative thought has blocked this goodness and it is just sitting there waiting to be let out.

─────────────

It is exciting to know that the more I listen to the chattering that goes on in my mind, the quicker I can identify the blocks to my positive and creative energy. Today I release all negativity so that I can be fully alive in the moment.

"The happiness of solitude is not found in retreats. It may be had even in busy centers. Happiness is not to be sought in solitude or in busy centers. It is in the self."

Sri Ramana Maharshi

No matter where I go, I take me with me. If I am agitated, my agitated mind keeps me company. If I resent someone, they accompany me in all my travels.

> If I am at peace,
> I feel peaceful
> wherever I am.

I begin my day with quiet time, finding peace and serenity in my meditation. I carry those feelings with me wherever I am. If anything happens to disturb this peace, I can stop and spend a few minutes with my breath and regain my serenity.

*Today I know that with every in-breath, I am
breathing in powerful healing energy. And
with every out-breath I am letting go.
I am letting go of all anxiety, all stress . . .
all negativity that is standing in the way
of my feeling good about myself.*

There was a time in my life when I hurt and I would do anything to make the hurt go away. Sometimes I felt so empty that I would do almost anything to feel full. And some days I felt so bad about myself that I would do almost anything to change that feeling.

There was a time when I thought that there would never be enough for me of anything good. When I found it, I wanted to grab it all at the moment, afraid it would go away. And I wanted to hold tight to anyone or anything forever that made me feel good for a moment.

There were times that I put things into my body and my life that I knew were not always good for me. If they let me feel good in the moment, that was all that mattered.

Today I look beyond the immediate moment of satisfaction and decide what is good for me in the larger picture of my life. Today I have faith and patience and can wait to make loving and positive choices.

I love the person that I am becoming.

Diane Crosby

"Only your mind can produce fear."

A Course in Miracles

Stop and think about this for a moment and you will never be the same again.

All feelings begin in the mind. They begin with a single thought.

Think a happy thought and you will feel happy.

Think about sadness and you will feel sad.

Think about a worrisome fearful thought and you will feel fear. Fear does not lie outside of you. It lies within you. No one can produce fear in you but you. Only your mind can produce fear in your body. Your own fear comes from your own interpretation of a condition in your life.

You have power over all your fear.

Today I will look at all my fears in a new light. I can now see them as a result of my thinking and will turn over all my fearful thoughts to my Higher Power. Fear no longer owns me or is a threat to my day.

*"Insanity is repeating the same things
over and over and over again and
expecting different results."*

*Change is an action step and I am taking
new action today to bring positive change
to my life. I no longer accept the unacceptable
ways that do not work for me.*

"Look lovingly upon the present, for it holds the only things that are forever true. All healing lies within it."

A Course in Miracles

Our past is but a memory in our minds.
Our future is but a dream in our minds.
Our NOW is what is happening in the moment.
All there is is NOW and I am at choice
as to how I feel about it.

Today I choose to feel love in this moment.
Today I choose to let love
fill my day and bring joy.

MAY 23

I do not need to know anything about this day beyond this moment. This moment is perfect . . . just as it is and I can handle anything in this moment. My Higher Power gives me all the strength I need today to handle whatever comes up in this moment.

MAY 24

*"Your heart will lead the way
to your fulfillment."*

Emmanuel

In the process of recovery, we heal our past. With this healing, our past will no longer be the predictor of our present. Because something was one way once does not mean that it will continue to be that way as long as we are willing to change. As we become willing to give up our addictive personalities, we are no longer ruled by fear.

This leads to the process of faith, first in a power greater than ourselves, then in other people and then gradually . . . oh, so gradually . . . we begin on that beautiful journey to trusting ourselves.

*Today I dare to believe in the beauty of love.
Today I trust that I am being led to love
by love and my day will be full of love.*

I celebrate myself today. I am alive.
I am growing. I am willing to do all
I am able to do to be the best of who I am.

"Security is mostly a superstition. It does not exist in nature, nor do the children of men as a whole experience it. Avoiding danger is no safer in the long run than outright exposure. Life is either a daring adventure, or nothing."

Helen Keller

Avoiding change does not automatically guarantee me security. Avoiding risk and danger does not mean that I am even safe. So much of life outside of me is outside of my control.

My real security lies within myself and my contact with my Higher Power. As I come to trust in the goodness and strength within me, I will be able to be alive and present to all that life offers with less fear and more faith and excitement.

Today I know that I am being guided and protected by a power greater than myself. I look forward to the unknown around the next bend in the road, the adventure over the next hill.

"The miracle comes quietly into the mind that stops an instant and is still."

A Course in Miracles

When my mind is racing and arguments continue in my head and will not give me peace . . .

All I have to do is stop.

Whatever I feel in this moment will pass.

All I have to do is stop . . . and breathe in and out . . . in and out.

And as I bring my attention to my breathing I will begin to feel peace.

I will take all the time I need
to keep in touch with my Higher Power today.
Meditation slows me down and
brings me peace whenever I choose.

MAY 28

Nothing can stop me from feeling wonderful
today. I am filled with all the wonder
and splendor of the universe and
I pass these on to everyone I meet.

"A clear light seems to fall upon us all—when we open our eyes. Since our blindness is caused by our own defects, we must first deeply realize what they are. Constructive meditation is the first requirement for each new step in our spiritual growth."

Bill Wilson
As Bill Sees It (Letter, 1946)

When our minds are busy planning, thinking, remembering, judging, resenting or any of the hundreds of other things that our minds so automatically do, we are too busy to see who we really are.

Meditation is the quieting of the mind. When we meditate, we can look within and see our truth. In this quiet we can begin to discover our defects that have been blocking our path.

———————

Today I will be gentle with myself as I meditate and look within. I will look at my inner self lovingly and without judgment as I find the blocks that have kept me stuck.

*I am putting a large stop sign
to all my negative self-talk today.*

It takes great courage to go in new directions. It takes great courage to try things that others around us have not tried.

One can have courage while one has fear. Courage does not mean the absence of fear. To open new doors, to take new steps while walking through our fear takes the greatest courage of all. Each new door opened gives us confidence to open the next door.

By trusting the goodness within us and going beyond the fear, life is an exciting, satisfying and fulfilling place to be.

healthy me!

Today I continue to remove any barriers that
keep me from being fully who I am in this universe.
As I continue to trust my inner guidance,
I receive all the inspiration I need
to grow in courage and faith and love.

Change means letting go. Change means giving up. Change means making the space for something new to come into our lives. Change means taking action.

If we think we have to make all our changes ourselves, it can be very frightening. But as we develop more and more faith in ourselves, in our friends and in a power greater than ourselves, we become less afraid of change. As we become more and more willing to let go of what is negative and destructive in our lives, we begin to find that we have the strength and courage to do what we need to grow in a positive direction.

Today I know that my Higher Power
gives me all the strength that I need
to move forward. I can feel this strength grow-
ing within me as I dare
to take one new step at a time.

"Today I know that I cannot control the ocean tides. I can only go with the flow. Today I can learn how to float to the top and let myself be carried buoyantly, joyously through life. When I struggle and try to organize the Atlantic to my specifications, I sink. If I flail and thrash and growl and grumble, I go under. But if I let go and float, I am borne aloft."

Marie Stilkind

Today I choose to go with the flow.

This morning and evening I will take the time that I need to be still and hear God's will for me. This thought alone brings me peace. This commitment brings me serenity.

This day is full of miracles. They are right in front of me on my path. Today I have the courage to let go of all that is holding me back so that I step forward and experience each miracle that is waiting for me.

JUNE 5

Today I know that I have everything I need.

There is not one thing that I need in this moment that I do not have. When I really know that, my struggle is over. As long as I know that all my needs are being met, there is nothing to fear.

When I live this day in the moment, being fully in the NOW, I feel complete.

Peace and relaxation flow through me
with every breath that I take.
I am complete in this moment.

JUNE 6

"If I feel that my pain has in part been occasioned by others, I try to repeat, 'God grant me the serenity to love their best, and never fear their worst.' This benign healing process of repetition, sometimes necessary to persist with for days, has seldom failed to restore me to at least a workable emotional balance and perspective."

Bill Wilson
Grapevine, March, 1962

I know that I cannot be hurt by anyone if I consistently look for their best. Today I continue to search out the best in all my relationships, looking for something I can love in everyone.

Life is not always comfortable. Life is not always free from pain.

There was a time when we would do anything to avoid discomfort and pain. We would reach out to our addictions and compulsions and obsessions to numb any feelings we didn't want. We would fill ourselves with people, places and things and then, if that didn't work, we could escape unpleasant situations by not being there.

Today if I am uncomfortable, I know that there is something that I can learn. And I know that I don't learn anything by running away or not showing up.

Today I am willing to experience all my feelings without hiding or running away. I am feeling alive in all moments and I am living this day to the fullest.

*"At some point we care with all our heart . . .
and we finally let go. We give it all we have . . .
and trust the rest to God, to Nature, to the
Universe."*

Ram Dass and Paul Gorman

Before I knew any better, I either tried to control everything or I gave up my control to others, thinking I could control nothing.

Not only have I learned that controlling everything is impossible, but today I do not even want to do it. Today I want to be well and heal and grow. And this can only happen when I trust and let go.

---

*Today I do all the footwork I can to
make my life work. I trust the results to God
and know that they will be just
what is good and right for me.*

JUNE 9

I am discovering who I am with joy today.

Today we might be asked to do something that might make us uncomfortable or take us away from our sense of security. It might require courage. It might require putting the feelings of another first.

Today we can care about other people in our lives. We do not always have to come first. We can do for others, even when it means giving up our comfort and our time.

We can let our hearts give us answers when our heads might shout NO. We can come from a place of love and find to our surprise that we are filled with a new softness and gentleness, a new sense of purpose and personal satisfaction.

Today my heart brings me to new places of giving and sharing that I have not yet experienced. I am a friend today and get great satisfaction when I put the needs of others first because I want to, not because I think I have to do so.

JUNE 11

As I dare to look within and discover what needs to be changed in my life, I can slowly begin to take the necessary steps to grow. I do not have to change my entire life today. I can make one change at a time.

Each small change gives me the confidence to make another one and then another one. Each one gives me the strength that I need to move forward.

Today I have the courage to look without fear at what needs to be changed in my life.

Since nothing living can remain unchanged, I can choose to make any changes within me positive ones. As a result, I can look forward always to more growth, more change, more love, more life.

Today I will honor my own values and
be open to change as a result of growth.

"Recognize that no matter how many times we get what we want, it always passes."

Jack Kornfield

Everytime we thought we found what made us happy, it eventually changed, became less meaningful or fulfilling. Everytime we thought we had arrived, there was always another road to take, another hill to climb.

There will always be something else that we want and somewhere else to go. That is life. It moves and changes and never stays the same.

Today we are learning that we already have all that we need within us. We are discovering our connection with the spiritual energy of the universe, that we are one with God and each other.

I am open to experience my connection with God and all the people I meet on my path today. There is new joy each time I realize our sameness rather than our separateness.

JUNE 14

So many of us had parts of our childhood that were painful and unpleasant. In order to escape, we often lived in our imaginations and dreamed of days in the future when life would be different, when it would finally be the way that we wanted it to be. This was the only way we thought we could have any control of our lives . . . when we grew up . . . when we would be in charge.

As long as we continue to think we will be happy in the future, we will never be happy in the moment, and that is the same as saying that we will never be happy. If we think that our lives will be better when we get that better job or retire, stay or go, gain or lose weight, or when our children grow and leave or come back, we are putting off the happiness that there is in today.

It is exciting to know that I am in charge
of my life today. God gives me all the faith
and courage I need to be present and aware
in each moment and the wisdom
to see what needs to be done.

JUNE 15

Things do not always turn out the way we want. Life can take strange and disappointing turns that are often out of our control. Floods and blizzards, heat and cold, along with stock market fluctuations and world events, just to name a few, can change the course of our entire outer lives.

When thoughts come up that remind us of times when people, places and things did not work out in a positive way for us, stop and sit back and take some quiet time. Remember the good that you have done, the kindnesses given and the love shown to others.

A smile, a sharing of the joys of the sunrise and sunset, perhaps teaching a small child to ride a bike or fly a kite . . . these are what counts in a lifetime. The time taken to push a swing, help a neighbor, write a letter, send a card . . . the giving of ourselves in a way that money can never replace . . . these are the things that will always be remembered.

Today I will stop and remember all the times that I gave lovingly of myself and know that these were my successes. I am a very rich person when I understand that the moments that come from love cannot be measured on any scale. They are priceless.

JUNE 16

"Scientists tell us that our body is constantly rebuilding and curing itself. When the body is fed the mental picture of wholeness, it builds its cells according to that picture, whereas when fed thoughts of hopelessness and incurability, the body builds the cells according to that mental picture."

Catherine Ponder

Today I choose to see myself well and whole. Today I put all my energy into positive thoughts, knowing that my body is healthy and strong.

*I am learning new ways to deal
with all that comes up in my life today.
I am letting go of all negative ways
of dealing with stress and anxiety that are
harmful to my mind and body.*

*Today I will look honestly at what is real
without denial and judgment. I accept my
reality without struggle and this gives me all
the energy I need to deal with
what needs to be done.*

"... *conflict will inevitably arise so long as there is a division between 'what should be' and 'what is,' and any conflict is a dissipation of energy.*"

Krishnamurti

*Today I will look honestly at what
is real without denial and judgment.
I accept my reality without struggle and
this gives me all the energy I need to deal
with what needs to be done.*

*My past experiences no longer
take up room and live in my mind and body.
I am free to live in today.*

"Faith is the thread we hang onto when our life is falling apart."

Sharon Wegscheider-Cruse

Sometimes faith is right there, holding us up, keeping us light so that hard times feel manageable.

And other times we have to 'act as if' we have faith to get through the tough times. We have to pray for faith.

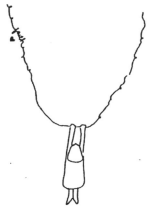

It feels so good to know that no matter what is going on today, I have the faith to know that my Higher Power is guiding and supporting me.

"If you compare yourself with others, you may become vain and bitter; for there will always be greater or lesser persons than yourself."

Desiderata
Max Ehrmann

No matter what happened in our past that appeared to hold us back, we can look today with gratitude that we have come this far. There might have been days that we were afraid that we would never make it. There were times that we thought we weren't good enough. There were times we thought others would go further than us.

Today we can know that our happiness does not depend on what anyone else does or how far anyone else goes. What counts is what we do with our lives.

---

*Today I know that I am not the best
or the worst. I am just me.
God is guiding me to become the best me
I can be and that is very exciting.*

JUNE 23

Stop and find a few moments alone today and sit quietly with your mind. Bring your attention to any part of your body that might be painful or tight. Imagine that accumulated stress and past experiences are held in those places. First picture them as solid blocks.

Now imagine them to be softening and becoming liquid. Now imagine all that liquid any color you like . . . any texture . . . any temperature . . . begins to pour out of those areas. Envision it pouring out of your body . . . from the tips of your fingers and from the tips of your toes.

Feel your body soft and gentle and flowing freely . . . released of all tension and all stored stress from past experience.

Today I am learning to release my stress and
anxiety in positive and healthy ways.
My body is becoming free from all negative
experiences. My past no longer
lives in my body.

*". . . Allowing yourself to be whoever you are
and wholly loving yourself for that."*

Ramtha

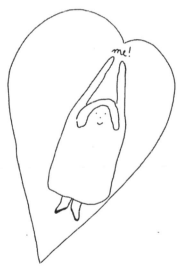

*I love me because of all that I am, not just a
part of me. I fully accept myself just as I am
today and that feels so good.*

"Many men go fishing all of their lives without knowing that it is not fish that they are after."

Henry David Thoreau

To spend one's whole lifetime waiting for life to come to us . . . thinking that if we just quiet our minds we will find peace . . . waiting for life to make us happy . . . could there be a greater waste.

That is not to say that serenity and peace are not found in fishing. They certainly are, as they are found in many other quiet hobbies and activities. And they are certainly an important part of life. But they are not what life is all about, not what we are to spend our lives looking for.

The beginning is in the quieting of the mind. That is just the beginning. As we quiet our minds our answers will come. And we will know what right action steps are to be taken.

Today I sit quietly in prayer and meditation so that I can hear God's Will for me. I know I am being guided in this very moment.

*"Setting others free means setting yourself free
. . . You become the victor instead of the victim
when you dare speak the word of release to or for
the person or thing you think is binding you."*

Catherine Ponder

When we hold a resentment, our entire mind, body
and spirit holds that resentment and responds to it in
negative and destructive ways. We remain stuck in
the past and continue to live with the feelings from
a memory, blocked from experiencing the present.

Willingness to release, to let go of that resentment is a beginning. When we forgive someone,
we are actually freeing ourselves from all that
tension and negative energy. It is something that
we do internally, not externally. The other person
need not even be present for us to feel the relief.

---

*Today. I am willing to let go of all the
resentments I am holding. My now is so
much more important than the burden
that I have been carrying from the past.*

JUNE 27

Today I am learning to be gentle with myself. Today I can look in the mirror and smile and know that I am okay just as I am. I am treating myself softly today.

"All problems fade out in proportion as you develop this ability to be quiet, to behold and to witness divine harmony unfold . . . "

Joel S. Goldsmith

My quiet-sitting meditation time helps me to develop new quiet times during the rest of the day. Today I can look at any problem I have and release its energy so that I can be free to allow harmony to unfold.

JUNE 29

*"Consciousness is like a river, and your whole self
. . . including every cell of your body is continu-
ously being fed by it . . . Just as your body lives by
the flow of blood that carries the substance of food
to every cell, so is your whole self being sustained
through the substance of thought emanating from
the flow of consciousness."*

Ramtha

Take a moment and think of someone you love.
FEEEL that thought with your entire body.

Take a moment to remember a time when you
felt hurt.

FEEEL that with your entire body.

FEEEL the difference.

Know that you are choice.

———————

*Today I am becoming more and more aware
that I can choose how I feel in the moment.
Today I choose to let go of thoughts
that are negative and destructive.
Today I choose to FEEEL good.*

Through meditation we begin to get in touch with truth. We begin to hear more often the conversations going on in our heads that we have reacted to most of our lives. By hearing these conversations and learning that they came from our past, we are then able to choose that we no longer have to react to them. We can begin to create new messages.

Today I will listen to the messages that go on in my head and decide for myself if they are healthy. Today I will choose to follow positive messages that I tell myself or create new messages that are positive and healthy.

JULY 1

"Seek always the answer from within. Be not influenced by those around you, by their thoughts or by their words."

Eileen Caddy

When faced with a decision as to which way to go today, I will pause and take the time that I need to feel it through. I no longer have to look to other people for approval. I can seek advice and then make my own decisions. I can take quiet time and go with my intuition. I can let my body tell me what is right for me.

Today I trust my instincts. Today I trust that I will know at the right time the right answer. Today I have the faith to know that God guides me in my choices.

I am accepting myself just as I am,
imperfections and all. I am not striving
to be perfect today. I only want to grow, to
change, to become more and more open
and let God and love be in charge of my life.

Many of us lacked consistency while growing up. Many of us received conflicting messages while growing up, depending on our parents and the mood or the conditions that they were in at the time. Many times we could do something one day and get praised, then do the same thing the next day and be punished or ignored. These mixed messages can keep us from feeling good about our decisions.

Today I can search my own heart and discover whether my intentions are positive or constructive reasons. Today I can trust that when I come from good and love, I am making the right choices.

JULY 4

Today I will find someone less fortunate than I and give them what I can. Today I will let go of my own troubles and self-pity by finding someone I can help.

"There, but for the grace of God go I."

But for circumstances, we could be someone else. Some of us were born to families with less financial resources than others. Others were born physically challenged. Some had fewer opportunities, lower I.Q.s, or less motivation or love. As little as we think we got, there were others that had even less.

For whatever reason we are where we are at this very moment, it is now within our power and reach to go forward. We never have to suffer the way some people suffer as long as we know that we are at choice, that we can turn to a power greater than ourselves for a life full of healing and love.

I am very grateful to be
exactly where I am today.
I do not need to be a victim of my past
or controlled by circumstances. I am in
recovery today and it feels wonderful!

"We perceive that only through utter defeat are we able to take our first steps towards liberation and strength: Our admissions of personal powerlessness finally turn out to be a firm bedrock upon which happy and purposeful lives may be built."

Bill Wilson
Step One, the *Twelve and Twelve*

When we admit that we are powerless, we no longer have to struggle on alone. Whether we ourselves are addicted to something, or we live or work with an addict, or have been affected in any way by an addict, there is a place for us to heal and recover. No matter what the addiction is, there is a twelve-step recovery program for us.

———————

It is a great relief to know that all I have to do is turn to the twelve steps of recovery and help is with me. Today I am given all the tools that I need and am so grateful that I no longer have to struggle alone.

The power of love transcends
all other forms of human power.

Barbara M. Thomas

To be powerless but still so filled with power—
this is the divine contradiction. Yet the total sur-
render of ourselves, body, mind, emotions and
spirit, creates the space into which Love's power
may flow. Armed with this power each of us may
walk into the tragedy of another person's life and
prepare space for a moment in time—a moment in
which God may enter.

Now expect a miracle in your own life, as well
as in that of your sister or brother.

Today I let go totally
and give God space to do his work.

Dis-ease in our minds can create disease in our bodies. As we begin to take more and more responsibility for our lives, as we continue to quiet down and look within, we discover the thoughts that are bringing us tension and uneasiness.

This tension is often caused by reliving old feelings. When we keep yesterday's experiences alive with resentments and by rerunning the old tapes, we are the ones that are keeping alive all the unpleasant feelings.

*Today I am looking within to discover what
I am holding on to from the past. Today I am
willing to let go of all old anger and resentments
that keep me stuck in tension and pain.*

JULY 9

Our mind used to automatically make comments on everything that happened. It was always judging, commenting, criticizing, approving, deciding whether something was right or wrong, good or bad, too big or too small, too this or too that. I was so busy comparing what was to what I thought it should be or wanted it to be that I did not have time to enjoy the moment.

Today I am learning to stop judging
and comparing so that I can be with what is.
I am learning to accept what is without the struggle
of trying to decide whether it is right or wrong.

"Please, Lord, teach us to laugh again but, God, don't ever let us forget that we cried."

From a card
from Casa Serena

No matter how much we grow, we never want to forget where we came from. No matter how we succeed and change, we never want to forget our pain.

Our pain has a purpose. We did not go through it for nothing. The memory of our pain helps us to have compassion for those still in pain. We can share our pain with others and be a light for their recovery.

Today I will share my strength, hope and experience with someone still in pain.
I will serve as a power of example to someone who is willing to let go of his suffering.

JULY 11

There are times when you must "march to the beat of a different drummer, no matter how distant." Trust your instincts. Trust your truth. There will be times when it appears as if the whole world thinks differently than you. There will even be times when it appears as if you are alone and have no support.

Dare to go beyond appearances. Know that when you are coming from your truth, you will never be alone. Do what you have to do in your life, and peace and love will follow.

Today I look within to find my truth. I ask a power greater than myself to guide me and show me the way and all I have to do is follow. It is that simple.

*I am at choice today. I accept the responsibility
of my life with a new sense of maturity,
confidence and even excitement.*

"There is no winter harsh enough to withhold the promise of spring."

Karen Kaiser Clarke

No matter how badly we feel, it is only for now. When in deep pain or confusion, we often think it will be that way forever, that we can never feel better. When in the depths of darkness and despair, it can be hard to remember there will be light again.

There are so many lessons in the cycles of nature. Sometimes they might sound trite but truth *is* really that simple.

Dawn does follow night. Always.

Spring does follow winter. Always.

No matter how dark the night has been, no matter how harsh the winter has been, we, too, change as do the seasons.

I can go through anything a day at a time, a moment at a time with the faith and the knowledge that my Higher Power is guiding me to peace and security.

*Today I know that if I am coming from good
and love, then only good and love will happen.
Today I know that what I give, I receive back.*

*"Whether you think you can or can't,
you're right!"*

Henry Ford

*Today I choose to think positive.
Today I let my thoughts lead the way
to success and happiness.*

Whatever we feel, others feel. All our joy and our sadness, our hopes, our fears, our loves and our hates . . . all of them are felt at some level by all of us. When we know that we are connected in our hearts and in our spirits, we can never be alone again.

Be an ear to someone else today and feel how much you get back. Look for someone who needs to talk and experience a transformation taking place within you as your own problems become smaller.

This in no way belittles what you are going through. It just keeps us from feeling unique, self-centered and therefore isolated. It shows us that the world is bigger than where we live.

Today I am willing to give away what I need for myself. I am willing to listen to someone else's problems. That way we will both see that we are traveling together on the same journey and are not alone.

JULY 17

*God gives me all the answers I need
at the right time. Today I trust that it is okay
not to know everything and that
I will know when the time is right.*

" . . . *when you get to the places that you dread,*
you will find that they are as different as possi-
ble from what you have imagined . . . "

Hannah Hurnard

When we project our fears into the future, we are living in a world that we are creating in our minds. It is impossible to picture the future as it will be and our minds will certainly exaggerate our fears.

Reality is in the HERE and NOW. If we keep our minds in the HERE and NOW, we will have the energy to do the footwork that needs to be done. Once we know that we have done everything that we can, we can then let go with trust, leaving the results in the hands of our Higher Power.

Fears sometimes still linger in my mind.
I can be okay when that happens. I can feel them
through and talk about them and go on in spite
of them, not letting myself picture the worst,
but seeing the results in a positive light.

"Transformation is a journey without a final destination."

Marilyn Ferguson

As long as we are willing and open to change, we keep growing and growing and growing. And we grow at different rates and come to different depths of truth and peace and understanding. Often when we have settled into a time of understanding and serenity, something new might appear that stimulates new growth and understanding.

To continue to experience life can be a great joy or a time of fear. Here we can make the choice to go with faith into the unknown or continue to live with fear. To choose to let go of fear means accepting that we will never arrive at the place where we know everything. As long as we are alive, there will be something new to learn, something new to experience.

Today I have faith that I am being
led to the answers that I need to learn.
If I keep putting one foot in front of the other,
I will always be in a safe place.

"God constantly speaks to us through each other, as well as from within."

Thomas Keating

If we stay within ourselves trying to work things out, thinking we are the only one who can solve everything, we will struggle unnecessarily. If we wait to hear the answer directly from God, we may wait a long time.

When we are open to others, we will hear new ideas and new solutions. When we accept that we are all connected by love and universal energy, we can give up our lonely struggle. We will receive new energy and support and love.

Today I am reaching out to those
who love and support me. I am letting go
of my ego and self-centeredness
so that I can make space to take in love
and support and ideas from others.

*Today I am open to everyone who is on my
path, whether I know them or not. Somewhere
there will be someone who needs my help and
I want to be there for them. My Higher Power
will tell me what needs to be done.*

JULY 22

"It is the perpetual denial of conflict that leads to the compulsive behavior of any addiction. Not allowing ourselves to face and come to terms with what is really bothering us, we drive ourselves to focus elsewhere."

Margo Adair

Many of us reached outside ourselves to feel better. But better from what? Let us stop and look at what it is that we do not want to feel. Let us stop and see what makes us feel sick or negative or unhappy.

When there is unhappiness going on within us, the conflict will not go away until we face it. With meditation and prayer, we will discover our truth and get all the guidance we need to grow and change.

Today I am growing in my faith that I dare to look at what is really disturbing my serenity. Today I trust that by searching deep within for my own truth, I will discover the door to freedom and peace.

"But when there is love and beauty, whatever you do is right, whatever you do is in order. If you know how to love, then you can do what you like because it will solve all other problems."

Krishnamurti

Today I will put aside all negative and destructive thoughts so that I can come from a place of love. Today I will let go of all blame and anger and resentments so that my heart and my mind will be open and free to feel love and give love.

JULY 24

Today I am going to spend more time looking for all the positive things about myself. Today I recognize myself and acknowledge myself as a terrific human being.

"If you keep praying for a thing, it shows that you have not got the faith. You need only go ask once and then go ahead in faith."

David Spangler

*When I turn a problem over to my
Higher Power today, I will let it go with
the confidence that all is being handled for me.
After I have done all my footwork,
I know that the results will work out
just as they are supposed to.*

JULY 26

*"Until you can accept yourself, you lock the
doorway to the expansion you all yearn for.
This expansion comes through your heart. Be
kind to yourselves."*

Emmanuel

Be good to yourself today. Whatever you feel,
whatever you think is all a part of who you are. It
is perfect and until you can accept that, you will
stay stuck with your judgments. Resistance keeps
us stuck.

Be gentle with yourself today. Accept whatever comes up without judgment. Notice whatever happens, whatever comes up and simply
accept it.

---

*Today I will allow myself to just be
without judgment, without criticism.
I will accept all that happens
with love and gentleness.*

"Your health is bound to be affected if day after day you say the opposite of what you feel, if you grovel before what you dislike and rejoice at what brings you nothing but misfortune."

Boris Pasternak in *Doctor Zhivago*

When fear rules our lives and we hold in the truth of our thoughts and our feeling, our bodies become sick, as well as our minds and our spirits. Our bodies become storage houses for negativity and fear.

Once we can begin to let go of saying what we think others want us to say, we open our door to freedom. Once we stop projecting what we think the outcome of our truth will bring, we can be who we truly are and be at peace.

Today I release all thoughts and feelings that cause me harm. I am learning to put all fears aside and come from a place of truth and love. The rewards of this freedom are far greater than the negative results of my fear.

JULY 28

We used to escape by picking up a drink or a drug or by finding something else that would block our feelings, hide our pain. Today I know I can feel better by staying in the now, knowing that it is okay to feel all that I am feeling and make a conscious choice to feel better.

I have so many choices today. I can pick up the phone and call a friend, smell a rose, read a poem. I can reach out to someone less fortunate. I can take a nap, go to the movies or meditate.

I can even write a poem, make a movie or plant a rosebush.

It is exciting to know that I am at choice today
and that my choices are limitless. I can choose
exactly what I want to do to change
how I am feeling.

"Knowledge without action is the greatest self-con of all."

Sharon Wegscheider-Cruse

When we know in our hearts that it is time for change, fear often steps in and says stop. And our self-talk begins with all the old negative and destructive tapes like "I can't" and "It will never work" and "It's really okay just to keep things exactly the way that they are."

When this happens, know that these are tapes from the past, tapes that have played over and over again and have kept us from growing. They come from the fear that we might make a mistake, that we might not know what to do.

Only through action can we grow. Only through change can we heal.

Today I know that I am being guided and protected on my path for growth and freedom. All the positive energy in the universe is working for my greatest good. All I have to do is put one foot in front of the other.

"You may have habits that weaken you. The secret of change is to focus all your energy, not on fighting the old, but on building the new."

Socrates

The Way of the Peaceful Warrior

Take a good look at your life today.
Accept it just as it is.
Know that today is a brand new day.

Don't waste any energy on denial or regrets. If there is anything that you would like to make different, begin it now. Put all your energy into making a new beginning.

*I am developing new and positive habits today.
I am putting all my energy into moving
forward and building a healthy life.*

My heart is full of gratitude today.
I am free today to experience this day fully
and to follow my spiritual path.
I have been given a new day to live,
to grow, to give love and feel love.

"Forgiveness is a gentle refusal to defend our-selves against love any longer. It is a willingness to perceive everyone, including ourselves, as either expressing love or feeling a need for love."

Gerald Jampolsky

When we can see everyone as expressing love or needing love, we come from a place of love ourselves.

With this in mind, if it feels as if someone has harmed us and we are willing to forgive them, we will feel love, not pain or anger.

As we grow in recovery, we know that we are at choice as to how we feel. And as we become more and more willing to let go of old grudges and resentments and not accumulate any new ones, we experience how good it feels to feel love and we can choose this on a daily basis.

Today I choose to forgive instead of holding onto resentments. Today I choose to let go of all feelings that block me from feeling love. Today I choose to see everyone with the eyes of love.

AUGUST 2

"Every outer effect is the natural expression of an inner pattern. To battle only the outer effect or symptom is wasted energy and often increases the problem."

Louise Hay

We have created all that is going on in our lives. If there is something that we do not like, we must begin by looking within and asking ourselves what needs or attitudes we want to change. What are we willing to let go of so that our outer world is more pleasing?

When we change from within, our problems disappear.

Today I know that it is just wasting my energy to try to change people, places and things. By looking within, I can discover what really needs to be changed and then turn it over to my Higher Power to be released.

Today I will take enough time to do something good for myself only. I will buy myself a gift or spend worthwhile time doing something pleasant and fulfilling. I have enough time today and I deserve this time for myself.

"We have what we seek. It is there all the time,
and if we give it time, it will make itself known
to us."

Thomas Merton

Today I will slow down and wait for my answers.
I will stop rushing and struggling to find them.
They will make themselves known when I am
ready to hear them. By just knowing they are
here and that they will appear
in their time, I can relax.

AUGUST 5

"Try to find your own God . . .
as you understand Him."

Dr. Bob
Cofounder, AA

God, Allah, Higher Power, Creative Intelligence, a power of good . . . whatever we choose to call our power greater than ourselves . . . it does not matter.

This spiritual power is so personal that we can only be right if we feel good about it. No one can tell us how to pray, or to whom to pray. This power is the most personal thing that we have. It is not debatable. It is not right or wrong. It is not the God of our family, friends or country.

We come to know our own God and we will call it whatever we choose.

In quiet meditation I listen to my own Higher
Power today. I connect with my personal
spirituality in my own time and place.

AUGUST 6

"By swallowing evil words unsaid, no one has ever harmed his stomach."

Winston Churchill

How many times have you wished you hadn't said something? How many times have you regretted not waiting just a few minutes before opening your mouth?

In recovery we learn to be actors and not reactors. We learn to pause and take a breath and we learn restraint. We learn not to react to our buttons being pushed, and we learn that being right is not always the way to feeling good.

The question we can ask ourselves before opening up our mouth is, how important is it? We will feel so much better in the long run.

Today I do not need to say the first thing that comes into my head, or react to what others say to me. Today I can practice restraint of tongue and pen . . . think before I speak . . . and say kind things or nothing at all.

*"Always repenting of wrongs done
Will never bring my heart to rest."*

Chi K'ang

Let us let go of what we did yesterday and be free to live in the now. Whatever we have done cannot be changed. We can take whatever steps that need to be taken to correct any wrongs done. And then we can forgive ourselves.

*Today I will do all that I am capable of doing
at this time in my life to free myself of
past mistakes. And then I will let go
and live in my now . . . fully enjoying today.*

The peace that I feel in my life is growing richer everyday. As I continue to walk on my spiritual path to recovery, letting myself be guided by truth and love. Conflict is leaving, making more and more room for charity, serenity and usefulness.

"The problem is not that we too rarely fulfill our desires, but that we so often do, and are still left wanting."

Joel Goldsmith

The more we want what we do not have, the longer we will be looking to the future for our happiness. How many times did you think you would be happy when you received something or achieved something or won something? Yet when you finally did have it, you couldn't wait for something else.

Think about how many times you thought you would be happy when something happened and then when it did and you were happy, the happiness didn't last.

Today I will take the time and quiet I need to find that place of peace and happiness within me. Whatever happens outside of me will never replace that which I can find within me wherever I am.

"Historically speaking, when human beings are faced with the choice between destruction and change, they are apt to choose change, and it's about the only thing that will make them choose change."

Peace Pilgrim

Eventually some habits, relationships, ideas or survival techniques become outdated, no longer useful. We either outgrow them or we change.

If we do not let them go, not only will we be stuck, but we will get sick. Before this happens, it is important to know that we have a choice. We will see a time when our choice to hold on becomes more painful than our choice to let go.

Know that all it takes is willingness and we will have all the strength we need to let go of that which is destructive and negative in our lives.

Today I know that my Higher Power is guiding me through the changes that I choose to make in my life. I have all the energy that I need today to make these changes as easily and effortlessly as I wish.

I will take time today to stop and give a gift to someone needy, smile at a stranger or help a small child. I will take the time to do at least one thing that I usually find myself too busy to do, and I will inwardly smile at myself, taking the time to experience the feelings of my own kindness.

"So listen with your heart. That is where your Light is and your truth."

Today I am letting go of all judgments. I am releasing all negative emotions. I am quietly going within and trusting my inner spirit and I will know what is right for me.

"When one door of happiness closes, another one opens. But often we look so long at the closed door that we do not see the one that has been opened for us."

Helen Keller

Let us not spend anymore time looking at the past when we can do nothing about it. Let's do all we can to let it go . . . whatever that takes. We cannot move on until we do this. We could be losing many good opportunities because we are not looking for them.

Today is a day of opportunities.
I am open and ready to find them all,
knowing that I am receiving
all the guidance I need to move
forward and be happy.

Today I trust what I feel and I listen to my inner voice. It does not matter if it is logical or if others agree. My feelings and emotions guide me on a path that is right for me.

AUGUST 15

"Many persons have the wrong idea of what constitutes true happiness. It is not attained through self-gratification but through fidelity to a worthy purpose. "

As I become more gentle with myself, I am seeing others in a more gentle light. And as I am able to let go of my own selfishness and self-centeredness, I am becoming more and more compassionate to the needs of others. I am learning that I do have something to give and that I am useful.

As I grow in my ability to reach out, I am learning the joy of giving.

---

*Today I will spend some time putting my own
needs aside to help someone else.
It is good to know that I can be filled
with such good feelings and I get
so much when I give of myself.*

AUGUST 16

So often ideas we have established in our childhood stay with us long after they have any usefulness. Our likes and dislikes are influenced by reactions to those around us. We need to re-examine all old ideas and start over again, making new decisions about them.

living by my own rules

It feels so good to know that I am capable of making my own decisions and following my own path. My Higher Power is my guide and my inner voice is my teacher and friend.

"If you don't like who you are and what you are and what your world is reflecting, look to see what you are building and creating and what you have decided to accumulate or decided to make part of your life."

David Spangler

We are responsible for how our lives are today. Once we know this to be true, new doors of freedom are opened to us. We no longer have to wait for something to happen or someone to change. We just need to look around and make our own decisions about what we see.

———————————

Today I know that whatever is in my life
I have put there and therefore I can let it go
as well. Today I have faith and trust that
I can take an honest look at what needs
to be changed in my life.

AUGUST 18

Today when I feel rushed with too much to do and think that I will not have enough time to complete it, I will take the time to ask for guidance. I will pause and consider what is most important.

I will take a mini-vacation and meditate . . . letting go of all stress and tension, releasing all fear and doubt.

I will trust that my good instincts will guide me.

I have all the time in the world to do
God's Will for me today. I trust that my
Higher Power is filling me with all
the energy that I need for this 24 hours.

I value myself today. I value everything about me. I am finding people who value me as much as I value myself. I am attracting people who treat me with love and respect.

"Whatever you know, you will become. And when you begin to know all the things that are, you will become all that is, which is God, completely . . . the unlimited freedom and joy of being."

Ramtha

When you see yourself with limitations, your life becomes full of limitations. When you think that your happiness depends on other persons, places and things, you remain limited.

Today I am beginning to experience all that
I am, a unique and interdependent human
being. I feel complete and alive and unlimited.
I am free to experience love and joy.

AUGUST 21

God is guiding me in all my thoughts and plans and actions. I have given up all my struggling and self-defeating messages and have turned over all my thoughts to the power and energy of goodness and love.

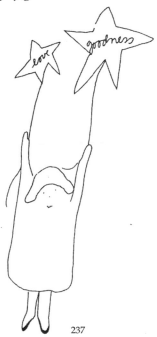

AUGUST 22

So many times we used to lean on others, rather than doing the work and taking the responsibility for ourselves. We often thought other people had the answers for us and so we sat back and let them make important decisions that concerned us. It was so easy then to blame them if things did not work out the way we wanted them.

Today I know that if I let someone else do my work, I am responsible for the outcome. Today I know that if I let someone take over my responsibilities, the responsibility for the results of their work is still mine.

Today I accept all the responsibilities
of my life. It feels good to know that
I am in charge of my life, that I am at choice
in my life and I can accept
the outcome of my decisions.

Everywhere I turn I know that I am being supported by powerful, positive energy. I am finding love and support wherever I go.

AUGUST 24

"The clearer the path, the easier it is to see the holes in it."

Frank Seymore

When we are in a state of confusion, it is hard to know what trouble is in our lives. It's like being on a narrow path full of twigs, rocks, stumps and holes on a black starless night. We keep tripping, stumbling and bumping into things. We get sore, cut and black and blue. And then we take another step and it happens over again. It will continue to happen until we shine a light on our path, see what needs to be cleared out and then fill up the potholes.

When our actions keep causing us pain, it is time to stop and look within. It is time to shine a light on our character defects and change.

I no longer want to repeat the same mistakes over and over again. Today I take the time to slow down and examine the source of my difficulties so that I can move on a clear path with freedom.

AUGUST 25

*I am so pleased with all the growth
that I am experiencing. It is okay to feel good
about myself . . . and I do.*

When the day comes that you might feel so tired it is hard to put one foot in front of the other, when all you have done seems to get you nowhere, that will be the time to just hang in there. That will be the time to just hang in there one more second.

That will be the day you will see a sunrise or a sunset or a rainbow or a smile from a little child and you will know. That will be the day you will know that it is not all about the struggle you have been up to or the results you want to get. You will know that it is all about being touched with the joy of this day.

It will be a day you will always remember.

Today I am open to be touched by love, by joy, by nature. Today I put aside all the happiness that I seek so that I can be free to experience the joy of this very moment . . . right now.

"Whatever we see as our 'self' must have a place of dignity in our own hearts and consciousness before we can become individualized as personalities."

Marsha Sinetar

The way we see ourselves begins with our earliest memories. It comes from the messages that we received from those around us. If we see ourselves in any negative way, we are letting these messages of others run our lives in a negative way.

It takes time to identify those voices and know that they are not ours. We need to take that time to know that no matter what and who we are, we are just where we need to be to grow and mature.

Once we can allow ourselves this respect, we can develop as individuals. Today is a wonderful day for this.

Today I am discovering who I am. Today I am becoming my person, worthy of developing all of me. Today I am beginning to know that I am okay just the way I am.

Today I am worthy of being gentle with myself.

I am worthy of it and I am going to give myself gentleness and softness.

I am developing a new habit of being softer with myself today . . . of not driving myself so hard.

Today I will drive myself less and know that my Higher Power gives me the energy I need to do what needs to be done in this day.

I will stop pushing myself as hard as I do.

I will stop for a moment and get renewed by the energy that I receive when I know that my Higher Power is holding my hand.

*Everywhere I turn I find positive
and loving people.
My heart is full of peace and love.*

Everything is awake today.
The earth is alive.

I am part of every movement, every breath, every flower unfolding, every blade of grass that is growing, every bird, insect, animal and human being. I am part of every color. I am part of all the water and the air and the sky and the earth.

Today I know I am one with this universe.

---

*It feels so good to be alive and to be part
of this universe. No matter where I am
in my life today, no matter what it is
that I am doing, I know that I am growing
richer and richer with love and with life.*

Today I am learning to take good care of myself. I am learning not to get Hungry, Angry, Lonely or Tired. I am learning to HALT. If I do not take care of myself, I will look to others to take care of me. I might reach out to my obsessions and addictions to feel better and I stand the chance of becoming self-destructive.

Today I choose to be constructive and respect my body, my mind and my spirit.

Today I respect my body, mind and spirit
and am taking care of all three. I am gentle
and nurturing, putting my needs first.
Only then can I be well enough
to help others with their needs.

"What we expect, believe and picture, we usually get."

Ruth Ross

We succeed or fail according to what we think we will do. Today is a good time to stop and explore all the negative tapes that keep us from succeeding. It is time to listen to our self-talk, our messages that push us forward, hold us back or put us on hold.

Today I know I am worthy of having success in my life. I am listening to what I tell myself with gentleness and love, putting a stop to any self-talk that does not make me feel good about myself.

All my needs are being met easily and effortlessly today. I simply turn them over to my Higher Power and do the footwork.

I can start this day over anytime that I choose just by a change of my attitude. If things are not going my way, I can pause and ask for guidance and positive energy and begin again.

If something happens that is disappointing or unpleasant, I do not need to let it spoil my entire day.

I can turn it over.

I can let it go.

I can move on from there.

I can take another positive step forward.

Today I will experience each moment to the fullest. I will do all I have to do to let go of everything that is blocking me from being fully alive in this moment. Each moment is unique, within itself and the less I carry with me from the previous moment, the freer I am to experience the joy of the now.

SEPTEMBER 4

Many times in the past we wanted to change how we felt so much that we would do almost anything to feel better. We would drink even when we knew it was poison for us . . . we would eat even though we knew it was an escape. Or we would gamble when we couldn't afford to lose, just for the thrill and excitement.

We looked for the highs in alcohol or drugs, sex or relationships or gambling . . . whatever it took to help us escape our reality. Today we see that high was short-lived and the bottom hit us hard.

Today we are learning that reality is not something to escape but something to live and learn from. Today we are learning that the steadiness or balance that we find within may not be as exciting but it is always there and it is healthy.

---

*I have all the strength that I need today
to accept the realities of my life. I am guided on a
path of learning and growth and healing.*

I am a terrific human being. I deserve wonderful things to happen to me . . . and they are.

". . . if we listen to the way that we speak to ourselves when we make mistakes, we may be able to hear whether or not we are nurturing or destroying ourselves and our self-esteem."

Marsha Sinetar

What do we tell ourselves when we make mistakes?

Take the time to stop and listen to your self-talk. Chances are there are times when you put yourself down, judge yourself and are unforgiving with yourself. Notice how many times you have a negative thing to say about yourself and to yourself. Notice if you can accept your imperfections or are you only satisfied when everything is perfect in your judgment.

Gently make note and then change your self-talk to a positive affirmation that will make you feel good.

Today I am listening to my self-talk with a gentle, non-judgmental ear. It is okay to make mistakes today. I am giving myself positive messages with permission to accept both my victories and defeats.

SEPTEMBER 7

"Fatigue makes cowards out of all of us."

Coach Vince Lombardi

When we push ourselves too hard, not nurturing ourselves and not resting enough, we certainly cannot be the best of who we are. It is easy to make mistakes and have accidents. Our judgment is influenced by our fatigue.

When worry keeps us up at night, our problems become exaggerated. Fear can enter easily into a tired mind. And when we are afraid, we do not have the faith that we need to move along our spiritual path with ease and confidence.

Today I am getting all the guidance I need to
take care of myself. I need not keep pushing
beyond my limitations. I am learning to listen
to my body and my mind, and rest
when I get the message.

I am exactly where I am supposed to be today. Everything about this day, this place, this moment is perfect. Everything about me is perfect in this moment.

"Our concepts of a Higher Power and God—as we understand Him—afford everyone a nearly unlimited choice of spiritual belief and action."

Bill Wilson

There is no right or wrong when it comes to spiritual beliefs. Whatever you believe is right. Follow what your heart tells you. Listen to your inner self. No one outside of you has your answers.

God . . . Higher Power . . . Love . . . Goodness . . . Allah . . . Jehova . . . whatever is right for you is not a debatable issue.

The world will be closer to peace when we can all accept this basic truth.

It feels so comforting when I trust my own truth. It is both powerful and peaceful to know that we are all at choice. Each and everyone of us is being led on a path to peace and love.

Peace is flowing through me everywhere today, pouring all over my mind and my body . . . releasing all my tensions and anxiety . . . emptying me of all my negativity and fear. I am being filled with peace and love and serenity.

SEPTEMBER 11

"The path of gradual relinquishment of things hindering spiritual progress is a difficult path, for only when relinquishment is complete do the rewards really come. The path of quick relinquishment is an easy path, for it brings immediate results."

Peace Pilgrim

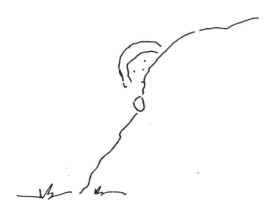

I am letting go of all that is holding me back from spiritual progress today. My path is becoming easier and easier as I open myself to faith and trust.

SEPTEMBER 12

Each step I take today makes me feel better and better. Today I know I have all that I need to do exactly what must be done and go exactly where I need to go.

"The elevator to recovery is broken . . . you'll have to use the Steps."

There is no easy shortcut to recovery. As much as we would like to see ourselves immediately healed completely, it all takes time. It takes doing it one step at a time.

And we can only recover one day at a time. Each day we are guided in our recovery from exactly where we are to where we need to go in this day.

If we can keep it this simple, we can enjoy this day . . . knowing it is the only day that we have.

Today I am taking all the steps that I can for
my recovery. My Higher Power is giving me all
the guidance I need, and I am full of joy
and gratitude that I am growing and healing today.

I am so grateful for the guidance I am receiving in my recovery. The more I open myself up to admitting I can't do it alone, the more I realize help is always there.

"It is imperative for our freedom to understand that our parents were doing the best they could with the understanding, awareness and knowledge they had."

Louise Hay

It is time to take responsibility for our own lives as of this minute. Whatever happened to us or didn't happen to us in the past is beyond our control. We can do nothing about it.

What we can do something about is to let go of any blame that we might have for our parents. We must be willing to forgive them for any pain that they have caused us so that we can be free. It is not even necessary to understand why they acted or didn't act in any particular way.

Today I am willing to take responsibility for my own life. I am willing to grow up and let go of my parents. I am filled with a sense of my own power and I choose not to give it away.

SEPTEMBER 16

*"If we are facing in the right direction, all we
have to do is keep on walking."*

An Ancient Buddhist Expression

There were many times that we did not know
where we were or where we were going.

On our new spiritual path we are walking
with our Higher Power. All we must do is continue as we are, asking for guidance from a
power greater than ourselves.

*Light is shining on my path today as I face
in the direction of love and goodness. One step
at a time it is leading me exactly where I need to be.*

SEPTEMBER 17

Today I continue to seek and find people who are positive, healthy and nurturing.

SEPTEMBER 18

"You must lose a fly to catch a trout."

George Herbert

Events of this day might show me that it would be better to let go of something I value than fight to hold on to it. This never happens unless there is something better for us in our future.

Letting go of one thing creates the space for something new to be able to move in.

When we give up the struggle, new prizes appear.

If something isn't working for me today, I am willing to let go of the struggle. I trust that God has something better in store for me.

"What is defeat? Nothing but education, nothing but the first step toward something better."

Wendell Phillips

Each time something does not turn out the way we would like it, we can use it as a lesson and grow from it. We learn from daily successes and defeats, always moving forward, always growing.

I grow and learn from everything that happens.
Today I am keeping my eyes open and my
head clear so that I don't have to make
the same mistake twice.

*I am very grateful for this day. I am grateful
for all the love and the inspiration that I receive
from my Higher Power whenever I ask. I just
stop and tune in to this universal energy and
am transformed to the level of my willingness.*

"Sunshine is delicious, rain is refreshing, wind braces us, snow is exhilarating; there is no such thing as bad weather, only different kinds of good weather."

John Ruskin

Today I am taking whatever comes in my stride.
Today I know that I can handle any change,
any surprise, anything at all as long as I remember
that my Higher Power is with me and
that I am never alone.

"Love builds highways out of dead ends."

Louis Gittner

Take the time today to remember a time in your life when you thought that life was all over for you. Remember a time when you reached a bottom . . . when you could go no further . . . when you were ready to give up . . . to quit.

. . . And remember what happened to turn that moment around. Was it an inspiration from a page in a book, a touch of a friend, a spiritual awakening?

Remember the love that was given to you, and how far you have come from that moment. It does not even matter if you are not where you think you should be . . . you are not where you were.

Remember the love . . . refeel that love . . . and pass it on to someone else in need.

Today I will find someone who needs my love.
Today I will share my strength, hope and experience
so that someone else can be reborn.

We can get so deeply rooted in the habit of telling ourselves negative things that there are times that we do not even know that we are doing it.

To bring awareness to the messages that you tell yourself, just for fun spend this day with an elastic band on your wrist. Every time you hear your inner voice with a negative message, snap the elastic band. It's hard to do this without smiling. Even if you feel foolish or silly or conspicuous, do it anyhow. Those feelings are okay.

And everytime that you snap the band, tell yourself a positive message. You will be amazed at the difference in your day.

Today I am really listening to the messages that I tell myself. Today I want to feel good. Today I am changing all my negative messages to positive ones.

Today I choose to do things for me that make me feel good about myself. Today is a perfect day to do something that I have been putting off.

"Today we can have a solid foundation on which to create and build a life based upon truth, choice and freedom.

"For years many of us were imprisoned by a multitude of mental blocks. Recovery is a process of transforming stumbling blocks into building blocks by working the Twelve Steps, utilizing a personal support system and relying upon God's gentle hands and guidance."

Joyce Suttill

Today I choose to build a pathway
to freedom from the bondage of self.

SEPTEMBER 26

*Today I have all the courage I need
to take the step forward in my life
that I have been putting off. I can manage
one step at a time, one change at a time,
with ease and with confidence.*

. . . We are going to know a new freedom and a new happiness.

The Promises
The Big Book

Freedom and happiness are not goals. They are by-products of a way of life that demands rigorous honesty and the willingness to grow along spiritual lines. Once the choice is made to live according to our truth, the path that follows seems so logical as to make us wonder why we took so long to decide to walk it.

Today I am living according to my truth, knowing that freedom and happiness are the result.

"It is no good hearing an inner voice or getting an inner prompting if you do not immediately act on that inner prompting."

David Spangler

When we know that there is something that we need to do to make our lives better, we can only feel better when we make a beginning on it. Delay Makes us feel very uncomfortable and eventually we will want to find an easier, softer way to take away that discomfort. We are in danger of reverting to old and destructive habits.

I am learning to trust my intuition and I am willing to act on this inner guidance. I am taking positive and healthy actions today and my life is getting better and better.

"The thing in us we fear just wants our love."

Marsha Sinetar

Be gentle with all your fears today. Do not beat yourself for having them. They are as much a part of you as are your talents and your dreams.

I love myself and all that I am today.
My fears are just one part of all that I am.
I am a human being on a progressive path to
recovery and every part of me is important
in the making up of who I am.

*I am one of the miracles of this universe and
I am connected to everything that was ever
created. I can pick up the phone or sit in quiet
meditation, choosing to make contact with a
friend or with my Higher Power or with both.
Today I know that I am never alone.*

". . . We have come to the point of our own bio-logical history where we are now responsible for our own evolution. We have become self-evolvers. Evolution means selecting and therefore choosing and deciding."

Catherine Ponder

As you read this page of your life, let yourself know how far you have come. Whether you have just picked up this book for the first time or whether you have been following it through for a while does not matter. Just know that you are at choice today and your future lies within your power.

Let yourself F E E E E L that power.

Let yourself K N 0 W the power that is yours. Give thanks for that power.

I am grateful for the power I have over the future of my life. I am being guided at all times to use my power with wisdom and love.

"What we create within is always mirrored outside us. This is the law of the universe."

Shakti Gawain

Whatever we see in our lives is a product of what is going on in our minds. Our thoughts produce the reality of our lives. When we live with loving thoughts, we find love all around us. On the other hand, if our mind is full of judgments, criticism, negativity or fear, that is what will present itself to us in our *now.* That is the way that we will find our world.

As I am learning to see the world through the eyes of love and compassion, I am becoming more and more full of love and compassion for myself and others. I deserve to feel good about myself today and I am learning how.

*I choose to be in places and situations
and with people where I feel good about myself.
I deserve to feel good and I trust that my heart
will tell me where to go.*

OCTOBER 4

"Peace is inevitable to those who offer peace."

A Course in Miracles

When confronted with conflict, we can choose to feel peace. When attacked in any way, we can make the decision not to fight.

We can come from a place of restraint and not act out in any hostile way, even if we want to. We do not have to act out our thoughts or emotions. We can pause and wait until we can come from our volition, from our choice.

We can choose peace.

Today I can wait until all negative
and hostile feelings lose their power over me
before I say or do anything. I can take the time
to breathe in peace and love,
no matter what is going on in my life.

OCTOBER 5

"Once you plant deep the longing for peace, confusion leaves of itself."

Seng Ts'an

We used to think that we would only feel peaceful when everything about us was better. And many of us found that that time never seemed to come. As soon as one problem was solved, another would pop up to take its place and the old struggle and frustrations stayed alive. The only way we seemed to be able to escape from all the chaos was to indulge ourselves, to block out our feelings with something else.

Today we can create peace in our lives by meditating, accepting what is and letting our problems go to a power greater than ourselves.

Taking the time to meditate keeps us centered and focused. When we come from a peaceful place inside, we create a peaceful world to live in on the outside.

Today I am developing a world of peace for myself, both inside and out. Today I know that I am always only one breath away from peace, one prayer away from serenity.

*"If I am I because I am I
And you are you because you are you,
Then I am and you are.
But if I am I because you are you,
And you are you because I am I,
Than I am not and you are not."*

Rabbi Mendel

*Today I am doing everything I can to totally
accept me as I am. Today I am doing everything
that I can to totally accept you as you are. I am
free to have an honest relationship
with me and you today.*

OCTOBER 7

I no longer decide what I should feel.
That is very limiting. If I limit my negative feelings, I
limit my positive feelings as well. Today I am opening
myself to all feelings. That gives me great joy.

"Fear knocked on the door. Faith answered. No one was there."

Anonymous

We do not have to live in pain and deception because of fear, shame and guilt any longer. When we become willing to dare to try faith, we will begin to know the joy of who we really are. Only then will we open to the love and joy that fear and shame had buried within us.

Today I am stretching myself and taking new risks.
Today faith is working to replace the fear
that has held me back.

OCTOBER 9

Sometimes it might feel as if you are taking a step backwards . . . or you are stuck . . . or have made no progress at all. Know at times like this that life has just stepped in to teach you a new lesson. Or maybe an old lesson . . . again.

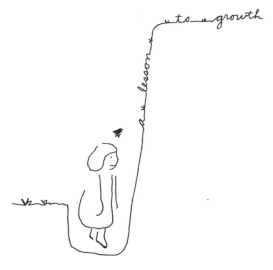

Today I am learning to trust that no matter what is going on in my life, I am in the process of growth.

*Today I will do something very special
just for me. I will treat myself to something
I want to have or do and feel good about myself
while I do it. My life is very important to me
and I have the right to be happy.*

Some of us have been brought up to think that we "should" place others before ourselves at all times. This is the way that they were taught and therefore that is what they had to pass down to us.

Today we know it is important at times to place ourselves first. We have a right to do good things for ourselves, have fun and feel good. Our lives do not have to be a sacrifice only so that others can be happy and succeed.

Today I know it is okay to place myself first sometimes. Today I am doing something very special for myself.

"I began to realize from a new perspective, that self-realization was the most painful but important search of all."

Shirley MacLaine

As we evolve as spiritual beings we can no longer point the finger at any one or thing outside ourselves. Our search automatically becomes more and more naturally directed inwards. We can no longer blame others for our discomforts or unhappiness.

At first this is not very pleasant. It is not any fun to find that we are at cause in everything. But soon we will see that this is the only direction to look in because we are the only person we can change.

I do not let pain or discomfort stop me from looking at myself in a true and honest light. I do not run away from myself today or block or disguise my reality. I face my life fully today to learn from its lessons.

OCTOBER 13

"Serenity is not the absence of pain. Serenity is reaching beyond surface appearances into inner truth, knowing God is working for our highest good."

Sandy Scotto Siraco

I am at peace today, knowing that God is doing for me what I cannot do for myself.

"It didn't come to stay . . . It came to pass on."

Seen on a Button

Whatever I am feeling will change. Wherever I am cannot last. Life is about flowing . . . no different than the change of night and day, high and low tides or the four seasons.

As they say about New England weather, "Wait a few minutes and it will change," so, too, our feelings and our circumstances are in the same process of change.

As soon as we really K N 0 W this, we will be able to take our lives much more lightly and ourselves less seriously.

I can accept whatever I am feeling today.
Without resistance my feelings pass and I am
then open to experience whatever is next.

I have a quiet place within me where I can rest today. I have a quiet place where I can go that offers peace, comfort and healing. It is as close as this moment . . . as close as a breath. This place is mine whenever I want it.

"No one can make you feel inferior without your consent."

Eleanor Roosevelt

How we feel about ourselves is truly our own choice.

We will never please everyone. Even to try is a useless losing battle. We can ask no more of ourselves than to follow our own inner voice, doing the best we can with each day. Then we are fine exactly as we are. We can be pleased with ourselves, and that is all that matters.

Today I am following my own inner guide,
knowing that I am coming from the best of who I am.
That makes me feel good about me.
That gives me great pleasure.

"The world would sleep if things were run by (people) who say, 'It can't be done!'"

Philander Johnson (amended)

We must be careful who we turn to for advice. It is important that we look to winners . . . positive and enthusiastic people who are not afraid to take risks, who are not afraid to lose. We can listen to their advice and then make our own decisions based on our own truth.

We must listen to our own dreams, our own inner urgings.

We will know inside when it is time to act. We will know inside what to do when the time is right.

Today I look to my Higher Power for strength, courage and direction. I gather my own strength and confidence from all positive resources and follow my own inner voice.

"to be nobody but yourself—in a world which is, doing its best, night and day, to make you everybody else—means to fight the hardest battle which any human being can fight, and never stop fighting."

e. e. cummings

Today we can put aside all tapes that come from others in our past and create our own new ones. Today we can clear out all the old blocks and find that wonderful person inside, that person we always wanted to be, that person that we really are.

We do not have to conform. We do not have to change. We do not even have to be liked. What we do have to be is ourselves.

The miracle of today is that we can love ourselves just the way we are. We don't have to be like anyone else.

I am full of joy in the discovery that I am okay just the way I am. Today I can accept all of me today, and that is a miracle.

I am so grateful that I have a power greater than myself to turn to when I do not have the answers. I am so grateful for the program of recovery that has brought me joy and purpose and love.

It used to be so difficult to face the truth that we built up thick walls of resistance and denial. Not only was it difficult to admit the truth to others, but we did not dare to admit it to ourselves. We were ruled by guilt and shame and embarrassment.

We might not have even known at a conscious level that we were in denial. We were so used to our rationalizations, we thought that our truth could do us harm. We didn't know that we needed to accept our truth so that we could move on and get well.

When we can finally accept ourselves, we will begin to heal. We can move on with our recovery. And then we can learn to love ourselves exactly as we are.

It feels so good to know that I am healing from my old wounds. As I bring love and acceptance to myself today I can watch the pain disappear and I feel so much better about myself.

OCTOBER 21

Difficult situations sometimes occur. Old patterns would ask us to escape or ignore them. Old patterns would put us in denial. Unless we deal with what life presents to us, difficulties will not go away. Any unfinished business will remain stored within us, waiting to be completed.

Today we can heal from unpleasant situations by just being present and doing the best we can. We can bring them to the best conclusion possible by turning them over and asking our Higher Power for guidance and direction.

Today I know that I am not alone. Today I know that God guides me in all situations and all I have to do to get help is to ask for it.

*"Was there something I was supposed to do with
my life?"*

Rabbi Kushner

If we keep on waiting until something happens for us to feel alive and full of purpose, we are missing out on life. If we keep on putting off moving forward, we are keeping ourselves stuck in needless misery.

---

*Today I pray for the knowledge of God's Will
for me and the power to carry it through.*

God is guiding me with every step
and every breath I take today.
All I have to do is wake up, ask for help,
guidance and knowledge to a power greater than
myself, and trust that I will know what to do.

When we hold on to anger and resentments, we block ourselves from feeling love. And when we don't feel love for ourselves, we can't give love to others. When we don't give love to others, we don't get love back. The getting does not come without the giving.

When we withhold love from others, we are withholding love from ourselves as well.

Anger and resentments hurt us more than anything else.

---

*Today I find healthy ways to express my anger
and resentments so that I can be free of them.
Today I empty myself of all anger and resentments
so that I can let love come into my heart.*

If I keep all of my time and my energy and love only for myself, I stay stuck. I stay limited. When I share my time, my energy and love with others, I find that I have enough for me and enough for them. I have more and more. It becomes limitless. The more I give, the more I get, the more I have.

No matter how busy I think I am, I will share
a part of me with someone else today. I am
discovering the joy of giving and I will take
the time to stop and share a part of me.
I am learning to trust the positive and loving people.

OCTOBER 26

I am learning to trust the
positive and loving people in my life today.

Sometimes you might have to "act as if" to push beyond feelings, to get to the other side of them where you really want to be. There are times when it is not appropriate to act out how you really feel. You might have to save those feelings and deal with them later in a more healthy and appropriate way.

Those times you might have to "act as if" you feel good, "act as if" you are coming from a place of love. The "acting as if" turns into reality when your intention is to get there.

When you "act as if" you feel love and are willing to go beyond the negative feelings, this creates new messages of peace and love and you do begin to feel it.

Today I practice restraint of tongue and pen and I do not hurt anyone intentionally. Today I give myself time to express myself appropriately. Today I go beyond negative feelings. I act as if I am coming from a place of love.

Today is a very special day. It is a day that I am going to be entirely me. I will begin by looking in my mirror and saying:

"Hi! I like you today!"

Then I am going to look within me and find out who I really am. I am accepting all of who I am today. Without doubt, without "If only . . . " *All of me.*

Only then can I see the part of me that is good and honest and real and loving.

And then without fear, I can look at the part that needs changing.

Today is a very special day.

————————

It feels so good to like all of me today. I feel warm and comforted in knowing that I am just fine . . . just the way I am.

OCTOBER 29

I am becoming open to loving others and letting myself F E E E L the love that other people have for me today.

"Today my happiness radiates from within me."

Gary Seidler

OCTOBER 31

"In our deepest moments of struggle, frustration, fear and confusion, we are being called upon to reach in and touch our hearts. Then, we will know what to do, what to say, how to be. What is right is always in our deepest heart of hearts.

"It is from the deepest part of our hearts that we are capable of reaching out and touching another human being. It is, after all, one heart touching another heart."

Roberta Sage Hamilton

Today I reach out and touch.

NOVEMBER 1

*It feels so wonderful to know that
I am truly full of goodness and love and
that I can begin from this very moment
to choose to express that part of myself.*

NOVEMBER 2

"According to the laws of aerodynamics, the bumble bee cannot fly."

There are times when we must go beyond all logic and take a chance with what we feel. These are the times when everything and everyone shouts *No* at us, and yet something deep inside says, *"Go for it!"*

We must go with our own convictions, our own conclusions. Life is too short for us to be led by the conclusions of others when we do not agree that they are right for us.

I am filled with all the strength and energy
I need today to follow my own truth. I am willing
to take risks today and find out for myself
what works for me in my life.

"The starting point for creativity is Silence ... the creative soil of silence, where can be found the seed-states of all things. Thus the first step in Right Imagination is Meditation ... then a form of direction will develop."

David Spangler

I will take time to be alone today.
I will take the time to be quiet.
In this silence I will listen ...
and I will hear my answers.

---

*In the silence of my meditation, I receive
guidance and direction. I am filled with all
the power I need to take my next step.*

NOVEMBER 4

When we find ourselves at odds with another person, we can choose to come from a place of love. We do not have to agree or give up any part of ourselves. Peace is not accomplished by saying something just to please. Peace is accomplished when we come from a place of love, say what is in our hearts, and accept that the other person is doing the same.

I speak from my own truth today.
I come from a place of love or I say nothing at all.

When old, uncomfortable feelings crop up, and I know that they do not have anything to do with the reality of the now, then I know that I still have some work to do on me. I have some work to do on letting go, some unfinished business that needs to be done. I must look within to make peace.

Today I am doing everything that I can to be in the now. That means letting go of all the baggage of the past that I am still carrying with me.

*Today I know that I am in charge
of the quality of my life. I am growing
in the ability to become aware of the
thoughts that have been controlling me.*

Today I fight for what is really important to me in a spiritual way. I no longer waste my good energy fighting to win or to be right.

There are some days when I wake up that I might feel light and full of JOY. On those days I might forget to turn my will and my life over to a power greater than myself. I might think that I can do it alone.

Other days I might wake up feeling heavy, burdened, full of worry. I might forget that there is a power greater than myself where I can turn to in this day and let go of all that is troubling me.

The stronger that I develop the habit, no matter how I feel, of beginning my day turning it over to God, the closer I am to finding peace and serenity.

When I get up today, no matter how I feel,
I begin my day by letting it go to a power
greater than myself. I am beginning this day
by giving myself the gift of prayer and meditation.

Today is perfect for whatever I choose to do as long as I come from a place of good and love. Today is perfect for me to be the best of who I am.

Today is perfect, one step at a time . . .
to feel alive . . .
to feel joy . . .
be open and caring . . .
to be fully alive and experience it all.

Today I am fully alive, fully open to feel all that there is . . . knowing that I can handle all that comes my way.

*"God grant me the serenity to
accept the things I cannot change,
Courage to change the things I can
And the wisdom to know the difference.
Thy will, not mine, be done."*

*In moments of stress, doubt, uncertainty,
anger or pain, I can pause and say the
Serenity Prayer, knowing that I will get
all the strength, courage and wisdom that I need.*

NOVEMBER 11

Recognize HOW FAR you have come TO-DAY. Recognize how much you have changed, how much you have grown. Recognize the good in you today.

It is a day to take positive inventory. It is a day to recognize your progress. It is a day to celebrate yourself today.

Today I am taking the time I need to look at my growth and progress. I celebrate being alive. I celebrate the good in me. Today I celebrate me.

Whatever has happened in the past is no longer in the now. The only way we can feel as if something is in the *now* is when we remember it. Then when our memory brings it to the present, our body responds with the same feeling as if it were actually happening.

There is no way that old memories can have any power over us unless we keep them in our minds. When we remember something that was done to us in the past, we are filling our *now up* with yesterday. We cannot be in the *now. It is* important that we let go of memories that make us unhappy so that we can be fully here *now.*

When I find my now full of yesterday's feelings,
I can ask for God to remove them. I can pray
to turn them over to a power greater than
myself so that they will lose their power for me.
I no longer need to hold on to memories which
create feelings that make me upset or unhappy.

Today I am looking within to discover what I am holding on to from the past. Today I am willing to let go of all old anger and resentments that keep me stuck in tension and pain.

"There was hardly a time that I thought that I wouldn't give life everything that I had. There certainly was a time that I thought that everything that I had was not enough. Today I know differently."

Ruth Fishel

Today I know that whatever ability, talents and energy I have are perfect for this moment. Today I know that God gives me all that I need to do what he wants me to do in this day.

"In the coming decades, the most important determinants of health and longevity will be the personal choices made by each individual."

Journal of the American Medical Association

Our body responds to our mind. If we have negative thoughts our body tenses. Our organs tense. Our bodies cannot function smoothly and in balance.

As we learn to think and act in a positive way, our bodies respond with health. The more we practice letting go of all agitation, tension, stress, anger, resentments, anything that is negative and destructive, the better we feel physically, mentally and spiritually.

Today I am learning to think and act in a positive way that is healthy for my mind, body and spirit.

NOVEMBER 16

"Faith is the time when it feels as if we are walking in hip boots knee deep through mud, when the fog is so thick you cannot see a step in front of you, and yet you know that you are being led and you are safe, one step at a time."

As remembered from Jim P.

Today I know that it does not matter if I cannot see the end of the road. I have absolute faith and trust that I am walking in the right direction and that I am being guided along the way.

There once was a time when some of us thought we could do it all, that something was wrong with us if we failed. Maybe there was even a time that we thought that if we said it differently, or acted differently, or stayed up longer or did it differently, the results would have been the way we wanted them to turn out. The results would have been the way we thought they SHOULD have turned out.

Today we know that we are not in charge of the results. Today we know that we just ask for guidance, do the footwork and leave the results to God.

Today I am doing the best that I can with
the guidance that I get. I leave the results to
my Higher Power and trust that they are
for the greatest good.

Let yourself know that as you walk through this day you are protected by all the loving energy of the universe.

Let yourself F E E E L a space of safety and love surrounding your entire body.

Let yourself know you are in a place where nothing can harm you, that you have all the protection you need to handle whatever comes up in this day.

Today I can handle whatever comes up, knowing that I am surrounded with all the positive energies of good and love in the universe.

I am so full of love and joy today.
I see it everywhere I look, and feel it
with every breath that I take.

"No 'What if's, no 'if only's, just LIVE . . . today."

Jane Drury

"What if's" and "if only's" keep us in the past. "What if's" and "if only's" replay old experiences, old memories, old tapes. They fill up our now so we can't experience it. Today let's tell ourselves that we have done the very best we could up until this very moment. Because we have.

There is not one thing we can change by looking backwards. There's not one second of history that could be changed by wishful thinking. We did all we could to get to where we are right now, and right now is perfect.

————————

Today I know that I have done the best I can with my life. Today I know that I am at choice and what I choose right now creates new memories. Today I choose to continue to do the very best.

*I trust God's plan for me today. I know that
I am being guided at all times. I know
all I need to know in any given minute.*

Self-pity is a very dangerous emotion. Self-pity blocks reality . . . it puts up walls so we cannot get positive messages . . . so we cannot even hear our Higher Power.

Self-pity brings us down to the far depths of despair and depression and neither of these are good companions.

When we think that we deserve to feel sorry for ourselves, and especially when we want others to feel sorry for us, we are indulging in negative thinking.

Self-pity leads us back to immaturity and irresponsibility, to wanting to feel better at any price, to the danger of returning to our addictions, compulsions and obsessions. Self-pity can lead us back to disease.

Today I refuse to allow the magnetic tape of self-pity to trap me. Today I avoid negative thinking and replace it as soon as I notice it is present in me.

"I am as my Creator made me, and since He is satisfied, so am I."

Minnie Smith

It feels so good to like myself today.
It feels so good to accept myself today.
It feels so good to know that I am exactly where I
need to be, doing what is right for me in this day.

"We usually feel emotionally we are hitting bottom but as we hit the bottom, we fall through a trap door into a bright new world—the realm of spiritual truth. Only by moving fully into the darkness can we move through it into the light."
Shakti Gawain

When we finally feel as if we are hitting bottom, that we can't do anything anymore, that we have no answers, the only way to go is up. At that point of our desperation, if we are finally willing to ask for help from a power greater than ourselves, if we have finally accepted that we need something beyond ourselves, it is then we can grow.

Once we know this simple truth, we no longer have to struggle on a daily basis. When anything comes up for us that is too great to handle, we do not have to hold on and keep trying alone. We can move through the darkness more quickly, and come to the place of light.

I immediately release everything that I am struggling with today. I release everything to my Higher Power, knowing that I am getting all the help I need today.

NOVEMBER 25

"We are all here to transcend our early limitations, whatever they were. We're here to recognize our magnificence and divinity no matter what they told us."

Louise Hay

Today is the day to clear out all remaining old messages that make us feel less than we are. Today is the day to listen carefully to hear if we still have any negative messages that block our progress to JOY.

Today is the day to see ourselves as the true and beautiful human beings that we are and celebrate ourselves.

Today I celebrate all of me exactly as I am.

*Today I am willing to let go of all the old ways
which keep me from growing on a spiritual path.
Today I am willing to push aside all the blocks
that stand between me and love.*

"Joy is the most infallible sign of the presence of God."

Teilhard de Chardin

Whatever your understanding is of God . . . whether it be a star or tree, Allah, Buddha, Christ or Yahweh, Good or Love . . . as long as it is a power greater than yourself . . . when you F E E E E L that power . . . when you K N O W that power, you will know JOY.

You will feel JOY in your heart. You will see it in the eyes of another human being. You will know it is greater than you and that you connected with everyone and everything in this universe.

Once you know this, you will never want to escape from the reality of your life again.

———————

*Today I choose to stay in the reality of my life and feel
all there is to feel. Today I am willing to feel
the pain so that I can feel the joy.*

*I know today that I am nothing alone. I am
willing to let go of any struggle that keeps me
on a path of doing things my way.
I know that all I have to do
is ask for help and it is there for me.*

"Yesterday has gone. Tomorrow may never come. There is only the miracle of this moment. Savor it. It is a gift."

Marie Stilkind

I am very grateful for the gift of this day.
It is mine to do exactly what I choose
and I choose to use it for good and love.

"... get yourself healthy. If you are healthy, you can do anything; the future is yours ... Working on yourself is the answer. Self-discovery is such a delicious life adventure."

Janet Geringer Woititz

At last we can discover how healthy it is to look within. We can finally put aside the curtains of fear and pride and find out who we really are. At last we can give ourselves the gift of truth and grow.

Today I know my journey to peace and serenity begins with me. Today I have the faith and trust to seek my answers from within.

DECEMBER 1

It is okay to feel exactly what I feel,
think exactly what I think
and even look exactly like I do.
Everything about me is okay today . . .
exactly the way that I am . . .
and this feels so very good.

I feel okay about me today and that is terrific.

DECEMBER 2

No matter what is going on in my life today, I can always find something for which to be grateful. When I stop and think about this and make a gratitude list, there is no room for depression or self-pity.

There is so much to be grateful for today.

Today I have a "gratitude" attitude.

I am beginning to trust myself today. There is a place deep within me that tells me I am okay and guides me along my path in recovery.

DECEMBER 4

Some of us have spent so long trying to be what we think we should be, what we think "they" wanted us to be, or trying to be who we would rather be, instead of just being ourselves. We have hidden from ourselves for so long. We have hidden our feelings in bottles and people. We have hidden from our fears and our truths, rather than looking at who we are. We have hidden ourselves from ourselves.

We were created on this universe to be ourselves. It is time to be and act exactly as we are. Only then can we begin to like ourselves as we are today. And the more we like ourselves, the happier we will be.

I am getting to know myself today.
I accept who I am today. I like myself today.

There are miracles in this day just waiting to be discovered. There are miracles waiting around every corner. There are miracles around every bend, and in every person that we meet.

There is the miracle of love and the miracle of forgiveness. There is the miracle of joy, the miracle of abstinence, the miracle of sobriety. There are so many miracles just waiting to be lived . . . a day at a time.

Today is full of miracles!

DECEMBER 6

*I feel lighter and better about myself
when I don't procrastinate. Today I am
discovering the freedom in completing
at least one thing that I have put off.*

"Life only demands from the strength you possess. Only one feat is possible—not to have to run away."

Dag Hammarskjold

There are days that we cannot always do what we want. Some days do not go our way. We cannot always play or have a "good time" when we want.

This does not mean that we cannot have fun in each day. Nor does it mean that there is no good in each day. There just are no guarantees that we will be happy every minute of everyday. Sometimes it might even feel as if the best we can do on some days is just get through it. What we do know today is that we can get through everyday without running away, without anesthetizing ourselves, without trying to block what we feel. And we know that these days will not last forever. It is just for today and we can do anything for just 24 hours.

Today I know that I can get through anything that happens in this day with the help of my Higher Power.

DECEMBER 8

*It feels so good to accept myself just as I am
today. All my thoughts and actions
and emotions are right where they belong.*

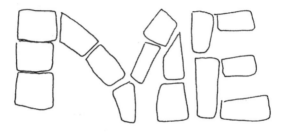

Today I know that in order for anyone to know who I am, I have to tell them. And in order for me to find out who someone else is, I have to ask. I cannot assume that anyone knows what is going on inside of me, nor can I read someone else's mind.

I have a right to have my needs met. In order to have them met, I am expressing them to the people who can help me today.

"Listening is a magnetic and strange thing, a creative force. The friends who listen to us are the ones we move toward, and we want to sit in their radius. When we are listened to, it creates us, makes us unfold and expand."

Karl Menninger

We all need a place to vent our emotions, a place to talk. When we don't have this, we live in our own heads too much and things become out of proportion. We lose our perspective.

It is so important to have positive and loving people in your life to talk to and with whom to share. In the safety of good friends we are able to release what we have been holding inside, freeing ourselves from negativity and fear. This frees us to be more open and grow.

Today I trust the positive and loving people to whom I am attracted. Today I am free to share from my heart, knowing that what I say will be treated with love and respect.

DECEMBER 11

The world cannot change overnight, nor can I.
Just one step at a time, one day at a time, I am
exactly where I need to be to get to exactly
where I am going. I trust this process today.

"A healed mind does not plan. It carries out the plans it receives by listening to Wisdom that is not its own. It waits until it has been taught what should be done and then proceeds to do it. It does not depend on itself for anything except its adequacy to fulfill the plans assigned to it."

A Course in Miracles

There is something special waiting for me to do with this day. I know that when it is time, I will be inspired from a place deep within myself. I trust that I will know what to do when the time is right.

Today we are learning that it is safe and healthy to open up and talk about our feelings . . . share them with someone else . . . release them.

The more that we are willing to open up to another human being, the more we will be able to see and the more that we see, the more we will find and the more we can release. We can release ourselves from the burdens of the past. We can empty ourselves from all our negativity and guilt and pain. We can open ourselves up to make room to become filled with peace and love, gratitude and joy.

Today I am willing to begin to share all of me with another human being. I am willing to trust that. this process will free me from the burdens of my past. I am ready to let go.

DECEMBER 14

"We will not regret the past nor wish to shut the door on it."

The Big Book
Alcoholics Anonymous

*Today I can look back with love in my heart,
knowing that every moment, every experience of
my life has been necessary, valuable and significant.*

"Life is what happens to us while we are making other plans."

Thomas la Mance

If we are living in the future, projecting, planning and dreaming, we are missing out on what is happening right now in the moment.

Planning certainly has its place. Plan when it is time to plan. And then let go. Turn your plan over. Be here now!

Today I am experiencing all of my life.
It is exciting to be alive in each moment.

*"Thoughts and words create
our future experience."*

Louise Hay

*Whatever I am thinking right now is creating how I
am feeling. I turn to positive and loving thoughts
because I choose to feel good.*

DECEMBER 17

"When you've exhausted all possibilities, remember this: You haven't!"

Robert Schuller

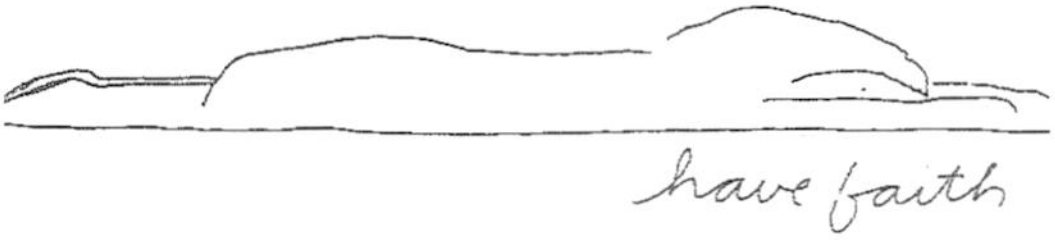

have faith

*When I have done all the footwork I know to do
and things are still not working out, I know
today that it is time to meditate. I have faith
that my answer is still to come.*

In order to be fully alive and participate in all of life it is necessary to feel ALL that we experience. We can't judge that some of our feelings are acceptable and others are not or choose what part of the day to allow our feelings to be felt, stuffed or denied.

When we stuff our feelings, we are pushing them down so tightly that they fill up all our spaces inside and leave no other space to feel anything else. And the more we deny our feelings, the less we feel.

If we deny our negative, painful feelings, we must deny our positive feelings as well.

Today I welcome all my feelings. Today I deserve to feel joy and love and gratitude and warmth and affection, just to name a few.

DECEMBER 19

"And let us always remember that meditation is in reality intensely practical. One of its first fruits is emotional balance. With it we can broaden and deepen the channel between ourselves and God as we understand Him."

Bill Wilson

As we develop the habit of regular meditation, our minds begin to quiet down and we feel calmer and more in balance.

In this quiet we are able to get in touch with inner knowing. Our own self-talk rests so that the messages of our Higher Power can reach us. Our own egos relax and with this comes truth.

In quiet and meditation I find emotional balance. I feel myself growing closer and closer to my Higher Power and I find love.

"A person does not make a conscious choice about becoming an alcoholic or co-alcoholic, and, without the intrusion of alcoholism, he or she would have made other choices."

Claudia Black

There is nothing we can do to change wherever our addictions, obsessions, compulsions and dependencies have taken us to this very moment.

It is important to acknowledge where we are right now.

It is important that we let go of any blame or guilt so that we can move on.

We cannot change our past. What we can do is make a decision not to repeat it.

Today I know that I am powerless over all the addictions, obsessions, compulsions and dependencies in my life. Today I am willing to let them go to a power greater than myself.

DECEMBER 21

*". . . the spiritual understanding of the individual
is the only understanding required for peace."*

Shirley MacLaine

*Today I seek spiritual understanding
beyond everything else.
I choose peace and love and joy as my goals.*

DECEMBER 22

There are days that do not always go the way we would like them to go. And we find out later that God's Will was not our own, even though we thought we were in complete alignment. When these days happen, as they will now and then, know that you are OKAY NO MATTER WHAT. That today is not forever, that everything changes and flows . . . that this 24 hours is just what it is in this moment. And that you can handle anything for a moment.

I can handle anything that comes up today . . .
even if it is only for a moment at a time.

As I start this day with quiet meditation,
I feel myself becoming still and at peace.
At any time during the day I can bring
my mind back to this moment. I will bring
my attention and awareness back to the peace
that I have when I am with my breath and
I know that my breath is with me at all times,
whether I remember it or not.

"The closer we come to the end of one thing, the closer we are to the beginning of the next thing. Birth and death, starting and finishing, filling and emptying, these are the processes by which the physical nature of life affirms itself. But the spiritual life never begins or ends, it just is. Only our awareness of it changes.

"Tending our spiritual life, increasing our awareness of it, and letting go more and more of our dependence on the physical part of life, is the way to real freedom and independence."

Sandy Bierig

Today I am learning to be increasingly aware of my spiritual life.

"Spiritual recovery is connecting again to life."

Judy Costello

*Love fills me and heals me as I open to connect
with the people that God has placed in my life.*

In the end, the only truth is our own, and the only success our own perception of it. We must walk our own roads, owning our own choices, valuing but not needing the approval of others. But at the end of our physical life, we will ask ourselves whether we are pleased with the way we spent it.

I live today as I want to remember my life.

"Much of what we know, both intuitively and rationally, is layered over by decades of learning to doubt ourselves and giving over much of our decision-making and creation-making power to others. By meditating we can go past these conditioned layers of self-doubt and discover our own wisdom."

Hallie Iglehart

Today I am unveiling all my layers of self-doubt and letting them go. Today I am taking back all the power that I have given to others by discovering the courage that comes from my own wisdom.

Today I am slowing down my pace.
I do not have to accomplish the entire world
in this day. It is one day. Today I have
time to stop and smell the flowers.

"Lord, give me the guidance to know when to hold on and when to let go and the grace to make the right decision with dignity."

Robert Schuller

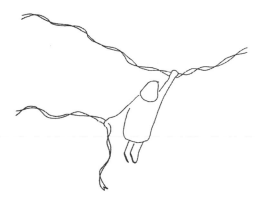

Through prayer and meditation, God guides
me to the appropriate people for guidance
in the important decisions I must make in my life.
I trust my answers to be there when the time is right.

"One thing I know: the only ones among you who are really happy are those who will have sought and found how to serve."

Albert Schweitzer

It feels so good to help other people and to know that I have something to give them. It feels so good to have turned my own life around so that it can benefit others.

DECEMBER 31

"Today is the first day of the rest of your life."

You have come such a long way to get to this point in your life today. You have traveled so many miles on a journey filled with so much, including sorrow and happiness, pain and JOY, defeat and victory.

Lay down everything that is a burden. And turn everything else over to a power greater than yourself.

It is time for PEACE.

It is time for LOVE.

IT IS TIME FOR JOY.

Today I know that I am at choice. Today I have all the willingness . . . all the energy and all the guidance I need to continue to choose the path of peace and love and joy.

PERSONAL NOTES

PERSONAL NOTES

MY PERSONAL AFFIRMATIONS

MY PERSONAL AFFIRMATIONS

MY PERSONAL AFFIRMATIONS